*Dear Sound of Footstep*

# Dear Sound of Footstep

## Ashley Butler

*So nice to meet you, i*
*Good luck with everything*
*in the future!*

*Truly,*
*Ashley*

Sarabande  Books

LOUISVILLE, KENTUCKY

No part of this book may be reproduced without written permission of the publisher. Please direct inquiries to:

Managing Editor
Sarabande Books, Inc.
2234 Dundee Road, Suite 200
Louisville, KY 40205

Library of Congress Cataloging-in-Publication Data

Butler, Ashley, 1980–
Dear sound of footstep / by Ashley Butler. — 1st ed.
    p.   cm.
    Essays.
    Includes bibliographical references and index.
    ISBN 978-1-932511-75-8 (pbk. : alk. paper)
    1. Butler, Ashley, 1980- 2. Mothers—Death. 3. Fathers and daughters. I. Title.
    PS3602.U866Z46 2009
    818'.6—dc22                    2008052598

ISBN-13: 978-1-932511-75-8

Cover art: "Cold Dark Matter: An Exploded View" by Cornelia Parker. © Tate, London 2008.

Cover and text design by Charles Casey Martin

Manufactured in Canada
This book is printed on acid-free paper.

Sarabande Books is a nonprofit literary organization.

The Kentucky Arts Council, a state agency in the Commerce Cabinet, provides operational support funding for Sarabande Books with state tax dollars and federal funding from the National Endowment for the Arts, which believes that a great nation deserves great art.

*for my mother and my father*

# Table of Contents

*Dear Sound of Footstep*

# *July 1999*

I've been watching the sky since 3:00 a.m., trying to pinpoint the moment when night turns into day. A lazy yellow strip of light wavers across the horizon, over downtown Richmond, VA, over Church Hill, past the train tracks, factories, and the James River. The yellow fades into a light pink, which then dissipates into purple, and finally an indiscriminate gray. I imagine industrial air clogging the machinations of early risers, wriggling into the corners of living rooms and over the lids of coffee pots, moving into yawning mouths not yet filled with words. A few stars remain, caught in atmospheric netting. The Annabel Lee idles at dock.

"Do you know why factories on the East Coast are built on the east side of cities?" my father asks me one day, driving back from a soccer game in Occoquan. He says the trade winds blow east, scooting noxious emissions over lines of houses east of downtown.

Standing between this forgotten colony and the window of this room in the Medical College of Virginia, the crown of Church Hill breaks the smog. On its slope, a playground with bright red and green aluminum slides and see saws remains deserted. At its base, trains slow, sigh, and heave along, past children chucking gravel at their wheels, placing nickels and pennies on the rails to be stretched into ovals. With closed eyes, they lean in along the rails. Tobacco row is quiet.

My father's house lies on the south side of Church Hill, next to a statue of a nameless Confederate soldier. I see my father, superimposed on a blue sky, in a vacant smile and full chest of air. In the spring, he says, everyone comes together to roast pork and dance at the *High on the Hog* festival. When he says this, I picture a red, cracked-skin pig turning over a black, crusted skewer, which runs between its thighs and out his mouth.

From the window of the hospital where my mother lies, I can see the bald spot on the southeast side of the hill where my father lives. It is the forty-acre emptiness devoted to the memory of a hospital called Chimborazo, which operated during the Civil War. During the War, it was referred to as the "hospital on the hill." The hill was chosen because it afforded good drainage. The name Chimborazo was inspired by a volcano of the same name, located in Ecuador. Although Everest is the largest elevation above sea level, due to the bulge of the Earth at the equator, the summit of Ecuador's Chimborazo is the farthest point from the center of the Earth. The distinction lies in point of reference.

Robert E. Lee, the Confederate General who surrendered at Appomattox while Richmond officials lay torch to the city granaries before themselves fleeing, was the first to find a figure in stone on Monument Avenue. His statue faces south, a sign of his safe return home. My grandparents found so much favor in his reputation that they named their son, my father, Robert Lee. They called him Bobby Lee. It's not a name I associate with my father. Years later, as he became careless in desire, I began to uncover the other names by which he went.

A few years after Lee's surrender at Appomattox, cardiologist J. M. Da Costa noticed the persistence of certain heart dynamics in Civil War veterans. There were alterations in the cardiovascular system, in blood pressure and pulse rate; there was a sustained exhaustion. They were jumpy, startled easily, were occasionally paranoid, and often saw things that were not there. They were indifferent to their surroundings, often confused past and present. Da Costa likened it to a sort of departure from reality, called it "Soldier's Heart." During the war, at Chimborazo, they used another term: nostalgia. Identified as a medical syndrome in 1688 by Swiss doctor Johannes Hofer, *nostalgia* was defined as the sad mood which derived from the patient's desire to return to a home that no longer exists. It was considered a curable disease.

I turn from the hospital window and look down at my mother's body. She is so small she blends in with the whiteness of the sheets. But the pattern on her nightgown gives her up: a colony of blue dots, row upon row. She would say that her love for my father, falsely received, made a lie of so many years. She would say it was "as if I never existed."

Even in her sleep she scowls, letting her cheeks, eyebrows, and twitching lips drop into their familiar creases. An IV clings to the wrinkled skin of one hand, while the other rests along her side. The other end of the IV travels up to a clear plastic bag marked

"Saline Solution," and hangs from a tall metal rod on wheels so my mother can take it to the bathroom with her, or on walks down the hall. When we walk down the hall she clutches the cool, metal rod for support. She smiles maniacally to quell the pain.

Halfway down the metal rod, a blue box is attached and beeping as a picture of two yellow lines monitors the vitals. Occasionally it beeps loudly and flashes a flat line across the screen.

Her blue dotted nightgown opens at the neck, displaying a catheter held steady by white tape. The catheter is a direct port-hole into my mother's jugular vein. Although she'd like to hide it, her clothes never fully cooperate. In old pictures of my high school graduation, my mother appears ghastly pale and skeletal for the middle of the summer, and her light green dress belies an altered terrain of flesh.

Before she began keeping track of my father's departure, my mother helped me build a model of Jamestown. "It will be like no other Jamestown in your class!" she said, and began lining up breadsticks for barricades. She stayed up the rest of the night to finish the fort. The next day I teetered into class, arms drawn wide by the berth of such fortitude.

My mother points to the white skin under her right forearm, indicating to me: "Look, all the veins have dried up." She smiles and sits straight up, grabs my finger and runs it up and down her arm, pushing down so I can feel the hardened strips no longer blue, all the while looking for a shocked response, as if to prove or make physical this impending death. She shows me the rectangle of raw skin on the top of her left thigh, where the doctors peeled off layers to graft the skin still remaining around the hole where her left breast used to be. The rectangle looks like an aerial view of a fallow crop field. The graft did not catch and when my mother lifts her left arm, I can see her insides. She would say, "Come, look into me."

I remember her head, half covered in a soft, blue do-rag I helped her pick out from a catalog of wigs and hats. They even had hats with hair built into them. The models in the catalog seemed to stare back with forced affect. My mother ordered seven wigs and three do-rags. Each wig came in its own cardboard box complete with mini-brush and pocket-size mirror.

Ordering clothes is easy compared to wigs. Or maybe we are not used to it. One wig is too orange, one is too small, and most just call attention to their manufacture. I try to convince my mother that bald is beautiful by citing a list of celebrities with recently bared pates. And when that doesn't work, I try to convince her to get a Bob Marley wig. When she still doesn't budge I go into her bathroom, pull on the orange wig and emerge. She stops crying and starts to smile. She would say, "I'm not ready to die; I'm ready."

Before she lost all of her hair, my mother let me dye it red. It came out brown and ugly. She laughed and cried. When clumps of hair started coming out in her brush, she told me to shave it off. That was the summer we went to stay in Savonnieres, a town near Tour, France; this was our last respite before death. She sat at the kitchen table, looking out through the overhanging roses to the garden. I got a white bowl, filled it with water, and dipped a razor in it. Bending her head forward, I considered where to start. The tendons behind her neck were pulled taut. I wondered if the blade would snap them in half, her head falling forward to clock her sternum. After each draw of the razor I dunked it in the bowl and watched the dark hairs spin. Time was in the languid swaying of wheat, the distant babble of the elementary school children, and

7

the calm, reassuring smile of the craggy, white-haired woman who always seemed to be standing in the doorway of her tiny house, her beagle asleep on the windowsill, and her blue print skirt lapping at the snatches of her ankles. This would be a nice place to die.

# Sea Vixen Heart
# Gloster Javelin

T o explore the edge of space, in the early 1960s, a pilot in the U.S. flew the X-15 to a height of 108 kilometers. At this point, the craft was considered a free-falling rocket with no aerodynamic control. As a consequence, "pilot" became "astronaut."

In the mid-1950s, an engineer named Theodore von Karman gathered a team of scientists to calculate the boundary between earth and space. After much time and consultation, the team decided on one hundred kilometers. It was considered a theoretical construction.

In 1951, they were the first jet-fighters of their kind to stretch into the sky. Among the better-known test-flight models were the ant, Dassault Mystere, Supermarine, Hawker Hunter, y Page, de Havilland Canada, de Havilland Sea Vixen, and craft descended from the Bell X-1, in which Chuck Yeager broke the sound barrier the same year the Central Intelligence Agency was born. Developed primarily for research purposes, this craft, the Bell X-5, was also known as the first aircraft to employ swing-wings—moveable arms—which were later found to send a pilot into an irrecoverable spin.

In 1951, the Sea Vixen was a two-seat, all-weather, missile-armed aircraft; the Gloster Javelin, an interceptor. The Vixen was designed as a high-speed jet fighter; the Javelin was designed for night operations. They had both been blueprinted to replace the post-war, single-seat, jet-fighter-bomber known as the de Havilland Sea Venom. The Venom had replaced the Vampire, which had been fitted with the new Ghost engine that once upon a time proved more powerful than the Goblin. The Vixen took to the sky two months prior to the Javelin. And, in the end, engineers and military personnel agreed on the Javelin for its cheaper and simpler design.

A year later, at the Farnborough Air Show, the Gloster Javelin was among the first ever display of delta winged aircraft. Following the Javelin's performance, before a crowd of thousands, the Sea Vixen broke the sound barrier, creating a triple sonic boom that shook the insides of spectators on the ground, and as the pilot prepared to pull into an upward roll, the aircraft, daring, disintegrated in the sky, felling the body of her pilot through the air, so near the clouds he fashioned his own impression on impact. The figures below shaded their eyes and looked up into the black masses of two descending Avon engines, which left a shallow depression filled with twenty-nine bodies.

Uncertain of what to do next, organizers cued the Hawker Hunter, which was finished in duck egg green though many witnesses later claimed as black.

In 1959 a man fell for forty minutes through a cumulonimbus cloud. He survived the impact but a pattern of the zipper from his flight suit remained imprinted on his chest; as if he might later undo himself, peer into a Plexiglas-cased heart. Of the descent, he later said, "It seemed like I fell for an eternity."

# *Les Nuages*

5:00 a.m., December 29, 2004. A tiny cockroach painstakingly makes its way across the folds of my comforter. I crouch to bring a bloodshot set of eyes to its wanderings and wonder how I look, all eyes, to this neophyte. Where there's one that small, there must be a mother and more not far. I search in the sheets, under the bed, in the cracks in the floor. I come across my mother's old spiral, the one with the cover decorated with rows of green watering cans. Inside, the pages begin with names and addresses then quickly trundle on. The handwriting changes from my mother's to mine to the nurse's—it's a diary of observations alongside a record of the drugs she was taking up until her death.

.   .   .

*"Où es-tu maintenant,* Ashley?" *Where are you?* My high-school French teacher often asked. I was thinking about clinical trials, the angiogenesis inhibitor. It was a treatment that would cut off the blood supply to my mother's errant cells. Unfortunately, it was *not a viable option for metastasized cancer.*

*"Je suis dans les nuages."* . . . *in the clouds.*

Madame Rimbault's lips would curl into a sly smile as she threw her head back and brushed the white strands of hair from her forehead. *"Faites attention, oui? Oui."*

"discomfort, lower spine"

4:00 a.m., Saturday, July 24, 1999. In my room with its blue carpet, walls, and ceiling, my sister, Hunter, and I try to nap. At 4:01 a.m., Katherine, the oldest, appears in the doorway. She is silhouetted by the light from the hall. The distance between our mother's breaths is about forty seconds. She says, "It's time."

The smell of rotten eggs, raw flesh, and feces is so strong it seems to seep into our clothes and skin. Rosemary, the personal nurse, places a sponge beneath the hospital bed and turns on her heel. She suggests we say our goodbyes now and pats Katherine on the shoulder in passing.

The body lies naked among the tangled white bed sheets. Long, white feet lean to one side of the bed. Right leg dangles off the edge. The veins that have not hardened can be seen to wrap throughout.

"Denies pain."

Left arm is swollen with lymph edema. I used to try her patience by pressing my fingers into her forearm, forming a crude shape of my name. As I watched the skin slowly expand to fill the relief, she would turn her attention to me with a patient disapproval: "Stop playing with my arm." It was a way of getting her to come back to me.

The jaundiced skin left on her chest clings to her ribs. Where her left breast should be is a hollow filled with regenerated tumors that have resurfaced over each other. These tumors look like red exploding puffballs with yellow spheres of pus implanted in concentric circles.

"2:40, oxycodone."

I glance at the containers of pills lining her bedside table.

"I don't have to do this," she said once, then added, "Is that what you want?"

"*Où es-tu,* Ashley?" I hear Mme Rimbault's voice.

Tumors spread from the left breast, up and over the shoulder, onto the back and down the spine, which has cracked. Above the right breast is a contour of the catheter against which the skin of the neck stretches.

The tumors continue up the neck and spine to the brain. The head is awkwardly angled back and to the side. The yellow flesh of the face pulls at the cheekbones and eye sockets. Eyes are half open, revealing the lower whites of eyeballs. Mouth hangs open to reveal rows of decaying teeth as well as a tongue black with rot, which I am supposed to continuously dab with a cotton puff soaked in lemon. Breath is that of a rotting body. I had promised not to let her die this way. It was a thoughtless promise.

"applying duragesic patch. 3 days"

Katherine takes the camera from the wooden chest in the living room. She peels back the bandages, wrinkles her nose and squints into the viewfinder. It is a close-up. It is ugly. The lumps have character. They are more alive now than our mother. They thrive on the blood drawn toward them.

"sleeping soundly"

Bedside, now, I take a light blue hand and place it on mine. A chill runs down my back and I have the impression she is grasping my hand. The hand is heavy, clammy. I am instructed by the nurse to tell her: "It's okay to go." And I do.

The oxygen machine in the corner responds with a rhythmic *kshh*.

For the next hour Katherine, Hunter, and I sit and wait and stare, hanging on each rasp, counting the seconds between, which seem to jump quickly from fifteen seconds, thirty, forty-five, fifty. Finally she inhales and we inhale, but she does not exhale. Katherine checks her watch.

5:12 a.m., Saturday, July 24.

I feel vaguely cheated. People do not die on the inhale. Exhalation is a sign of relaxation, almost acceptance.

Time seems distorted. Or, a part of me remains in the quiet, slow motion in which she dies again. I am guided by the shoulders, out of the room. Unable to grasp the extent of what is happening, I glance back, over my shoulder, to get one last look. But a paramedic in a black and orange outfit is folding the door closed and just beyond him I catch a last glimpse of another man similarly outfitted, leaning over her. I wonder how they will hold her, bend the knees against the chest to fit the bag they've brought.

Katherine, Hunter, and I crowd into the small meditation room built by the priest who lived and died in the house before my mother and I moved in. My mother's doctor sits opposite and talks in a soft, murmuring tone. "This should never have happened," he says, "Everything was done. This should not have happened." His head hangs down, arms heavy in his lap.

I deliver the cockroach to the window. Despite the occasional sound of a taxi the room is quiet.

> *"Où es-tu maintenant?"*
> *"Je suis dans les nuages."*
> *"Tu dois reviendre quelque jour,"* she says, *you must return some day.*
> *"Oui, je le sais. Je retournerai. Quelque jour."*

# *Bridge*

I am standing in the middle of the road, halfway across the Manhattan Bridge. The last rays of the sun are smeared down the sides of the skyscrapers in Tribeca. Over my shoulder, I can see the police. Their NYPD squad cars are angled toward me, red lights turning across my cheeks. Twenty yards away, a young policeman is closing the distance between us with long deliberate strides. I turn back to the sunset. Then he takes me by the wrist.

On the afternoon before Independence Day, on the second floor of a warehouse in DUMBO, Brooklyn, three bells sound within a six-minute interval. At the first bell, a green button lights up, indicating the start of a new round. I can just hear the beeping as I round the corner of Front Street and begin climbing the stairs to the gym. Inside, on my way to the small women's locker room in the corner, I pass by shadow-boxers and watch as they hunch over eight-pack abs and sneer at their reflections before releasing their fists into the air. When the bell rings again the noise in the gym climbs higher until, finally, the third bell sounds for rest.

After three hours of boxing, I crash on a mat and look up to see the sunlight fill the windows above, so bright that the gym hazes over, and I fall back into the memories I have come here to shake. Almost a year has passed since I last spoke with my father. He had been still unwilling to admit the truth: that he had stolen money, lots of it; that he had years ago stopped loving my mother; that he had started another relationship and refused us this information for the seven years she lay dying.

I had moved in with him during my second year in college, thinking if he could only confess, it would somehow make things right. I remember his hands—thin, wrinkled, and covered with brown spots. And I remember being eight years old, watching him work a wild strawberry root from our backyard garden—his hands were so large they seemed to have swollen the lines from his palms.

The last time I had seen him was through the eyehole of my apartment door. Usually he dressed in blue sandals that crisscrossed his pale, hairy feet with their yellow overgrown toenails, and gaping shorts that revealed legs so thin his kneecaps seemed to round them. But on that day, he wore a black suit, and a gaggle of tiger lilies trailed from his grasp, as if he had come to court, then put to rest, the image of the dead wife he sees in me. He stood outside my door, his head fallen toward his chest, as if too large and heavy for his frame. I rested a hand on the doorknob. He glanced up at the eyehole, then placed the flowers by the door and left.

. . .

After twenty minutes on the speed-bag, I unwind the wraps from my hands and stretch out the palms by forcing my fingers back. I drape my T-shirt along the window ledge to air out. Then I bound down the steps and out into the afternoon sun, hoping a short jog along the waterfront will clear my head.

I remember how, at the final bell of high school, I would change into my running shoes and sprint past the classrooms, basketball courts, and gym, through our Tarrytown neighborhood in Virginia. I jogged over the highway, behind St. Paul's Church and through the woods filled with rusted sinks and porcelain toilet bowls, to the edge of the James River. I stripped down to my underwear, dove in, and moved my toes through the mossy bottom of the river bed. Across the river, atop rocks smoothed by the water's way, cormorants perched like veritable gargoyles with their chests puffed up, wings spread out to dry and their black feathers glistening in the sun.

I am jogging under the Manhattan Bridge overpass. Construction is being done on the area where the road ends and the East River begins. A mid-size Caterpillar idles, abandoned in the late afternoon sun. I let my eyes linger on the impression the machine has left in the ground and consider how an absence could take on force. I sit cross-legged on a piece of concrete by the river and watch the sun spackle light across the water's surface. I let the sole of one shoe rest on the water and feel the slight buoyancy push back. I remember the brown sunspots on my father's cheeks and imagine the rays of sun burrowing down into his skin. And I imagine the doctors excavating these sun points with silver scalpels.

My father tells himself a story. He says, the trips were for business. He says, his wife stopped loving him first. He says, good Lord, I worked long hours for her, for the family. He says, I sacrificed. He says, people lie. He says, in the future, human beings will all look the same; there will be no black, white.

Slowly, I push one foot under. The East River is chilly. I let my body continue down, sinking my other foot and easing in to my chest. I imagine the river a toxic, neon green; imagine it somehow sterilizing my body as I slip in.

I see a ladder on the support leading up to the Manhattan Bridge. A few short paddles and I reach up to grab a rung. Leaning back, I set a foot on the first rung and pull myself up. The water parts in a web along my skin as though shrinking from itself. My black boxing shorts cling to my thighs and my skin smells foul from the river's lingering detritus. I feel the water suck me back as I pull away.

Light blue paint from the ladder chips off in my palm before peeling away with the breeze. I feel as though I'm on autopilot—here is the next rung, a series of holds. I don't think about the ways in which this climb could unravel, about slipping on still wet soles and falling fifty feet to shallow water or concrete, about getting picked off by a Coast Guard or NYPD bullet and falling one hundred feet, or about making it to the top, the underside of the road where a jackhammer methodically chips away at the asphalt overhead.

Two thirds of the way up, I glance over my shoulder, a hundred feet in the air, looking down on seagulls. In the center of the park that flanks the East River in Brooklyn, a giant boat with a plastic navigator's wheel rests, slightly tilted, in a playground. In the grass, a few yards away, a woman and child face each other and toss an inflatable disk that flies high, then turns sideways and slices through its descent. Looking down from the ladder, I feel like a small animal clinging to the back of its mother.

The ladder leads to a hole that has been cut through the bridge road. The jackhammer staccatos nearby. I contort my body to squeeze through the hole and peek up like a prairie dog. The subway runs along the far side of the road. Ten men in orange vests mill about beyond the jackhammer. I pull myself up and onto sturdy ground. I want to place a palm on the mottled pavement to gain evidence of its stability but I don't. I brush the asphalt and dust from my shoulders. The man with the jackhammer has noticed me and stops. I ask the way to Brooklyn and he points.

I turn around and start jogging. I try to convince myself it will be okay. I will go back to the boxing gym, back to the A train, back home to my apartment on the street that follows east to St. John's Cathedral with its right tower still covered in scaffolding, like some reconstructed limb.

But a red pick-up truck with the construction site overseer pulls up alongside me and I stop. "Where did you come from?" the overseer asks.

"Through the road. I climbed up the bridge."

"How'd you get through the road?"

"There's a hole over there."

He speaks slowly, softly, does not raise his eyebrows. "Well, just hang out here for a minute." He reaches his hand out the window and clamps my bicep. "Don't worry, it'll be alright, just hang out for a minute." He directs his voice, hushed so I won't hear, into a walkie-talkie.

Goose bumps cover my arms. After moments of silence in which I wonder whether I can outrun the pick-up, weaving through potholes, back to Brooklyn, my voice cracks. "I'm scared." The overseer pauses, and then says, "I know."

The police cars arrive. The young policeman closes the distance between us with long deliberate strides. I turn back to the sunset. And then he takes me by the wrist. He whips me around, claps the handcuffs onto my wrists. He directs me by the cuffs, pushing me ahead, into the back of the squad car.

Three minutes later, an ambulance trundles onto the bridge and I am transferred into the back. The sun is low in the sky now, no longer reflecting off the grid of skyscrapers. The ambulance doors shut.

I stand in a windowless, octagonal holding room. It is empty except for four policemen—two guarding the doors, the other two on either side of me. "Take off your watch and shoelaces." I hand them over, afraid they will make me strip down until I am cold and naked.

Instead, they grab me by the shoulders and push me forward as the steel door opens slowly. The hallway is lit by a dim, blue-white light. The tiles on the floor alternate black, white, black, white.

The policemen leave me in a chair. A doctor with a white lab coat and a gruff tone enters, tosses a light blue top in my lap and shows me to the female dorm, which is an empty room with three rolling cots. There's no door, and windows line the wall to the main room, in the center of which the nurses' station sits, abandoned. I lie down cautiously on the cot closest to the windows, wrap my arms around my torso, and let my mind wander to a more endurable reality.

I remember the weekends in New York, two years ago, when

my father and I walked around downtown. We went to the antique booths on Sixth Avenue where he liked to admire Venetian glass. Then we bought tiger lilies and groceries, returned home to cook kale and vegetable soup. Mornings we read the newspaper, cooked eggs, and I dragged him to bookstores where he waited outside. In my mind, the days were ideal.

My sister has always been the one who explains the things I don't remember. She would say, "Dad was always pulling pranks. You remember that time... well I guess you weren't alive yet but there was this time we were crossing a bridge. I was always afraid of bridges and I got down on the floorboard screaming, 'Are we over? Have we crossed the bridge yet?' Dad stopped the car and said, 'Yeah, we're here. Come on get out.' I popped my head up to get out and saw that he'd stopped the car in the middle of the bridge. 'We're all going to get out of the car,' he said, 'and walk around to take in this magnificent view.'"

When I ask my sister about moving on after loss, she says, "Try not to think about it. Try to think about the good times. The less you think about it, the sooner it'll go away and you want it to go away. You don't want to think about it." There's something about the way her sentences turn that brings her to peace and me to silence.

My father and I used to hike around the border of the eight acres of farmland our family owned in Virginia. He walked ahead of me, slowly placing each foot in front of the other as though measuring the line. I filled the divots his "duck boots" left with my Velcro sneakers. Circular bales of hay dotted the stretch of overgrown grass that crowded a derelict barn in the distance.

Ferdinand was the reason we were there. Ferdie, the bull that ranged, the bull I imagined breathing heavy air through his nostrils, tracking the length of this fence, searching for a weakness in the structure.

Every time he escaped and called on the neighbors, my father and I would drive out in his beige Buick with the blood stain on the backseat. The blood was from years ago, when I'd fallen off a wall and split my head on the asphalt. My father lifted my body from the ground, perhaps unthinkingly, in his impatience to heal me.

Arriving at the farm, we set out along the border to find the break in the track of barbwire. As we walked, I imagined the fence uprooting behind us and the landscape being pulled into the distance like fabric. If my father could see this, he might also dissolve before my eyes. If he could see this, I would pull a fistful of his yellow cotton shirt down and, in a voice unbecoming my frame, tell him not to look back.

"Yeah, I remember a bull," my sister says, "but I don't think it had a name. Wasn't Ferdinand the name of the bull in that children's story Mom used to read to all of us?"

"The one with the orange cover?"

From the window of the hospital, I watch the sun set in shades of pink and yellow across the sky. To the right, behind the square of low-rise buildings, a church spire reaches up to pierce low-accumulated smog. The cars have left the hospital's parking lot below—it was so full before. Just outside the parking lot, kids lope by the ten-foot fence surrounding the hospital.

I remember a question my father asked me once. We are driving to a soccer game in Virginia. It is evening and the sun angles through the pine trees along the interstate as my father and I speed along. Without looking up from the road, he says, "I've got a question for you. If you had a friend who wanted to use your eight-story high apartment window to commit suicide, would you let him?" I look up from my book. I wonder which one of his friends has asked him. But I don't know much about his other life. Over the years he has kept quiet about his lover, claiming it was my mother's decision to separate. I have wanted him to tell me everything, imagining that only then will I be able to know him.

"So what's the verdict?" he asks.

And I want to give the right answer, the one my father wants to hear. I watch as he drifts away. I try to lure him back. "How about you? What do you think?"

"Yes, I would let him." He keeps nodding as though there are things left unsaid, as though his thoughts go on, but this is all I am privy to. It feels like some dramatic moment so I don't speak. And I wonder if he is asking for permission. I think we'll never go fast enough. We focus on the road sprinting toward us and we watch the darker horizon blend with the ground that rises beyond.

# Light Rushes Past the Form
# To Which It Lays Waste

A woman is photographed before a sea. Behind her, bisecting the picture's plane, the horizon is presented by a line of overturned hulls or houses toward which the woman's elbows, waist, and right forearm converge. In her right hand, she holds a walking stick, which seems as though it may suddenly become an instrument for the distance that expands the small turn of a hand around the idea of a letter. And the camera hung around her neck, centered between her hips at the height where blouse and skirt tuck, where elbow bends the forearm in line with horizon and horizon divides the picture, is just another mark that reinforces both the site of a boundary and the sight of absence personified at a vanishing point. This inertia of order is also found in the constant deferral between sea and sky which never meet or make the horizon we imagine must be a curve somewhere always-already beyond sight. To rest in vision that veiling unveils a sea so blue only blood in hands is capable of making one felt from without.

Critic Urs Stahel's "On the Border" considers Seichi Furuya's photographic work with his subject and wife,

*a sense of desperation,*

*for the photograph remains a photograph and can never replace the individual, no matter how powerful and realistic the sign may be. Suddenly, the objects Christine made, the meal she was about to prepare, the fruit lying out on the table, all become material relics, almost sacred, to be photographed and filed away with her portraits in the visual archive of the mind's eye.*

We see Christine before the sea, pinned to this horizon, so deliberately centered in the composition that she seems to float like an entomologist's find, a distance boxed about the contour of her body, the safety a corner wants to promise, a rectilinear frame when placed in the context of a grid becomes one unit, the elemental. And because she floats we imagine the structure.

Snow articulates the line of a branch while ice blurs thin heightened extensions.

Of Christine's photographs, collected in *Memoires,* her photographer and husband Seichi Furuya writes—

*When possible I take the window seat on airplanes.*

*For a period of time after Christine's death, I only took photographs of the Berlin sky. The roar of the jet engine recedes and before long the landscape disappears.*

*We live as if encircled about existence.*

*This winter I experienced my first tremendous snowfall since living in Europe. Just as it seemed the remaining snow, turned to mud, would melt, it began to snow again.*

*In Austria people have the custom of building bonfires on the night before Easter. Only on this day is one allowed to burn the year's accumulation of fallen leaves and branches cut from trees.*

# *Stingray Point*

As the cornfields and tomato stands slide by the car, I squeeze the steering wheel with both hands and stretch my shoulders back. My eyes are tired. I sink into the car seat. Ten years ago, I would have been sitting in the back of the family station wagon, reading Roald Dahl and road signs, playing the name-that-vegetable game with my father, and leaning over the back of my mother's seat—feeling her hand on my cheek, pressing her face to mine. There were cornfields and tomato stands then too. We always stopped at the tomato stand right before the first bridge to West Point. Ripe red tomatoes, fried in the morning, on bacon lettuce tomato sandwiches at noon, and with mayonnaise at night. West Point 2 miles, Saluda 21, Deltaville 32.

In Deltaville, I take a left at the waterfront and ride by bobbing boat masts. The car ducks and turns up with the gnarled road; past the sailing school where I used to teach, past the loading dock where we backed our boats into the water, I turn off onto the crinkling grass in front of a gray-blue, vinyl-sided house topped with disposable shingles.

Inside it is warm, and smells of linens mildewed with bay water. One main room, surrounded by vertical crank-out windows, faces the Chesapeake Bay. Sliding open the glass door, I lean out to feel the warm bay wind blow my hair back into the house. It smells like salt and dead crabs. There is a swimming pool with a stiff, rusted diving board just outside the sliding doors. And twenty yards further down a hill of buttercups and pine cones, down seven splintery steps of scurrying sea lice, the black tar-speckled pilings stretch out to the sandbars and the setting sun.

Our family arrived in the evenings after stopping by Miss Lynn's Galley Restaurant for New England clam chowder, soft-shelled crabs with tartar sauce, and pink lemonade. I raced through the house, checking that everything was where it should be. My most prized finds: the bottom jawbone of a fish, a seagull spine, a dried up starfish, and one and a half sand dollars: all still under a bevy of cloth diapers in the back of a drawer otherwise filled with beach towels. And the horseshoe crab carapace I found washed up in the sand: neatly centered underneath the bed.

The dark interior of the house blends with the night. As a child, I placed fingers on the glass door and let them slide down slowly to make a high-pitched sound. With lips hovered by the glass, I blow warm breath to make a circle of condensation that lines up with the horizon which meets bay and sky in the distance. Then I draw a sailboat with a rudder so large it might capsize the boat.

Outside, Hunter would have tossed a towel on a chair and paused by the side of the pool before allowing herself to fall into the water. I imagine the surface undulate now, throwing back light from the half moon. The water's surface seems somehow more defined. Or maybe it is the sky that looks uncertain tonight. She touches the grate at the bottom of the pool then glides back toward the surface. She shakes a purple tie from hair that curves against the surface and, treading water, she looks up.

I wonder if she ascribes this sense of weightlessness to the space between the stars. Does she picture herself up there, looking down on this spot of water on the earth? The light on a sailboat mast blinks along the horizon. When I look back at the pool, she's gone under again, where hearing is distorted. In the afternoons, we cross our legs on the bottom of the pool, pinch fingers around imagined cups and lift our pinkies. In conversation we begin to lose our breath and we make up words. Our hair flies in all directions; we look as if we've just been electrocuted. Then we scream at each other as loud as we can; but it comes out high-pitched and weak.

At the far end of the house, in my parents' room, in the top drawer of their dresser, is a jewelry box made of popsicles. A rock is glued to the top for a handle. Next to it is a silver-colored hairbrush that my mother would rake through my "rats' nest" of hair after a day in the sun and salty water. Over their bed is a picture of my mother in a group of a hundred or more girls at summer camp. Second row from the bottom, seventh from the left.

In the attic, an angle of light illuminates the dust surrounding the neatly stowed cardboard boxes. Pictures of parties, couples, weddings, business trips our parents took to Alaska and Russia. My hands pass over them all and come to rest on one. In this photograph, my mother and I are sitting in an orange inner tube in the pool, caving in to the center, floating toward each other. There is the chlorine of the pool, my mother's skin, the mildewed inner tube. I remember the feel of my elbow pushing into her side, my shoulders cradled in the crook of her arm.

The sun sets, throwing a final lance across the bay. I focus on the horizon in hopes of seeing the green flash that I have read about. From the hall closet I grab a blue blanket and curl up on the L-shaped sofa in the main room facing the windows. Shadows of sailboats slouch past the horizon; stars speckle the sky.

In the morning the warmth of sunlight draws me from sleep. I walk down to the bay. Thirty feet out, a sandbar gently breaks the surface. With bare feet, I creep toward it, being careful not to step on any crabs half burrowed in the sand floor.

On the sandbar I stand with hands on hips and twist back and forth until my feet are lodged in silt. Stingray Point reaches across the left side of the horizon while Gwynn's Island reaches from the right. While the sun is warm the air remains cool.

Back in the kitchen I sip black coffee and watch the neighbor's yellow Labrador scoot past the fence that divides our yards. From the garage I grab a crab net, a six-foot wooden pole with a green nylon net gathered on the rusted end, and set out for the motorboat docks down the road. I walk barefoot, past the blueberry vines, which trail along a white fence by the side of the road. My mother and I used to walk out here with buckets and pick them.

The planks of the dock are worn and some of them are missing. I search for the Blue Crabs that cling to barnacles attached to pilings. It has a dark gray-green dorsal side, a softer bluish-white underside and the females have red lined pincers. The back two legs: flat like paddles with a consistency slightly stronger than that of an oak leaf. When faced with an opponent they stand still, sizing up the competition, then they scamper to one side, stop, assess the situation again then scamper the other way. When confronted they snap calmly, thoughtfully. And while their claws can inflict a noticeable amount of pain to human toes and other appendages, they can completely sever the arms and legs of other crabs. The trick in freeing them from garbled netting is to pinch their backsides, where their pincers cannot reach.

At the end of the dock a rope is tied to a piling and leads into the water. My father and I tied a rope here almost fifteen years ago. On the other end, underwater, was a two and a half square foot wire crab pot with a fish head in the center. The design is figured so that once the crab has found his way to the fish head he can no longer get out. But this rope leads to nothing but seaweed.

At night, the sound of an owl from the pines. The spring moon is heavy, full. The horseshoe crabs gather on the shore between the tidal lines. Or rather, the males gather and await the females who are almost twice their size. These females will emerge from the bay and drag the males across the half-buried piles of green eggs they have just released. Even from the seabed, two of the horseshoe crab's ten eyes are so sensitive to ultra violet that they will be able to detect the moonlight.

I walk down the hill toward the bay to watch their fossil-like frames intimate. The ebb and flow of water against the shore can sound like the swish of blood through the body. The water's surface looks like satin. The water feels tepid and gritty with plankton. The horseshoe crabs I expect to see along the shore are not there. A shell lies face down, unmoving, in the sand. I grab a stick and give the shell a nudge, then flip it over. The legs do not

flurry in the air. The shell shows no cracks. I pick it up by the lip
of its back and sand files out. I look for something inside, a sign
of a struggle maybe, or remnants of a body ravaged from its shell.
Neither is there.

# Let Our Craters Be Points Impressed By the Force of Imagining

"On the Moon, the new day does not trigger
the sounds of awakening..."
—Julius Schmidt, early sky watcher, 1856

The last man to walk on the moon took a sleeping pill the night before his departure. He slept soundly and dreamed he was navigating the Rover beyond the horizon. On the far side of the moon, he came across an abandoned vehicle, and some meters away, a person. As the figure turned, he saw himself pause, and look back.

Taken in 1959 by the Soviet Luna 3 spacecraft, the first grainy photographs of the lunar far side proved the terrain there more treacherous than that of the near. In the undulations of a surface felt initially by way of sight alone, visibility of two dark regions begged early names from the lips of scientists. Eyes squinting at grey designs, they named the regions *Sea of Moscow* and *Sea of*

*Dreams*. Then, after the return of the spacecraft, experts noticed a smaller region within the latter mare.

They called this the *Sea of Ingenuity*.

Ten degrees north of the *Sea of Ingenuity* lay Tsiolkovsky crater, named after Russian Father of Cosmonautics Konstantin Tsiolkovsky. Tsiolkovsky has been credited with several theories on human space travel and rocket propulsion. In works such as *Plan of Space Exploration* (1926) and *Cosmic Trains* (1929), he mathematically proved the possibility of space flight, including the design and construction of space rockets, space elevators, navigable rocket engines, multi-stage boosters, space stations, life in space.

In 1903, the year four lifeguards watched a Wright Brother launch his powered *Flyer I* off Kill Devil Hill and stay the height for a second shy of a minute, Tsiolkovsky published his classic *Exploration of Cosmic Space by Means of Reaction Devices.*

Here he established the basic equation for reaching space by rocket, a formula known as the "Tsiolkovsky Equation." It is an equation that includes a calculation of the escape velocity, or, the initial speed necessary to go from one point to infinity.

In *Research into Interplanetary Space by Means of Rocket Power*, he likened the state of weightlessness to the sustenance of a soaring bird:

>               *Sometimes the soaring flight*
> *of birds*        *prolonged*
>
>                              *indefinite span*
>
> *of time on account*
>
>                    *continual gusts*

*of wind      soaring*

*flight requires    thrust, without which          prolonged. In*

*birds, this   brought by beating    against    air   But*

*what if there are no such beats*

*if our bird were to stop still*

*in midst*

*of soaring*

*bound wings,*

*when hurled, hurtles*

*ground like stone,*

*as it would on Earth,*

*the force*

*like a boat*

*repulsed from shore in still water.*

An early biographer noted, in 1931, that, "Everywhere in all of his works, K. Tsiolkovsky demonstrates originality and ingenuity... on many questions he was ahead of European researchers, and in some cases he independently came to the same conclusions that were obtained abroad."

Born to a forester and housewife on September 17, 1857, in the small Russian village of Izhevskoye, Tsiolkovsky's life was altered early on by childhood disease. During the winter of his tenth year, after riding his toboggan for too long in the cold, he fell ill and became delirious. Doctors thought he would die; but slowly he recovered.

Tsiolkovsky later recounted, "I became very deaf and the deafness would not go."

As a result, he could not attend school. Instead, he took to

41

reading all the books in his father's library; and in 1873, the family sent sixteen-year-old Konstantin to Moscow where he studied mathematics, analytical mechanics, astronomy, physics, chemistry, and classical literature at Chertkovskaya Library under the tutelage of Russian philosopher and leading proponent of Russian Cosmism Nikolai Fedorovitch Federov. Federov believed that progress in science would allow humans to achieve immortality and resurrect the dead.

> *The signal given*
> *explosion touched*
> *off to accompaniment deafening*
> *roar. The rocket shudders and starts*
> *We feel as though we*
> *have grown dreadfully heavy*
> *I am thrown to the floor,*
> *shaken to pieces, perhaps*
> *dead            There are means*
> *of enduring*
> *this heaviness,*
> *wrapped.*

Under the influence of Federov, and Jules Verne's *From the Earth to the Moon* (1865), Tsiolkovsky began to consider designs of space crafts. At one point he thought he had discovered a way of reaching space by the use of centrifugal force. Of that night in Moscow, he said thirty years later, "I could not sleep. I wandered through Moscow, thinking all the time about the great consequences of my discovery. But by dawn I had already realized the error in my reasoning. That night left its impression on my entire life...I still sometimes dream of rising to the stars on my machine."

*This is the Earth we have just left.*
*It does not look convex, as if it were a sphere, but, in accordance with the*
    *laws of perspective, concave,*
*like a round bowl into the depths of which we gaze*

In his 1932 *Cosmic Philosophy*, in which he summarized his philosophical ideas on space civilization, Tsiolkovsky predicts the first space flight will signal the beginning of Space Culture in human history; it will, in fact, be the beginning of a new history.

Twenty degrees east of Tsiolkovsky crater lay Gagarin crater. On April 12, 1961, Yuri Gagarin was recognized as the first human to travel into space. From orbit he announced, "I looked and looked but didn't see God," and hummed a patriotic tune called "The Motherland Hears, The Motherland Knows." Composed by Shostakovich in 1951, the first two lines read: *The Motherland hears, the Motherland knows / Where her son flies in the sky.*

Eleven degrees north of Tsiolkovsky crater lay Wan-Hu crater, named after the man who first attempted to use a rocket to launch into the heavens. A Chinese official during the Ming Dynasty, Wan-Hu is said to have attached forty-seven rockets filled with gunpowder to a wooden chair. Perhaps, he thought, a weapon of war could supply the power for this long voyage. Wan-Hu sat in the chair, surrounded by a crowd of onlookers, as servants lit the forty-seven fuses and recoiled. There was a loud bang. Wan-Hu was nowhere to be seen.

In article after article of the three volumes titled *Collected Works of Konstantin Tsiolkovsky,* published by NASA, Tsiolkovsky invites:

*Imagine you are standing on a viscous soil, something like pitch so the soles of your feet cannot possibly adhere*
*Imagine a stationary building containing different objects that are also stationary*
*Imagine a small bench with a horizontal shaft; two wings are mounted symmetrically*
*Let our projectile be given the shape of a soaring bird frozen in mid-flight*
*Imagine two stationary, separate and totally unconnected bodies*
*We should not be unduly afraid of the enormous oppressive force of gravity*
*Imagine two motionless bodies existing close to one another*
*Everything is so quiet*

In a 1911 critique of Tsiolkovsky's theories, editor Blagonravov of the scientific journal *Herald of Aeronautics* noted that, "The mathematical arguments on which the author bases his subsequent conclusions give a clear indication of the theoretical feasibility of the idea. But the difficulties, unavoidable and enormous, that surround the extraordinary and unfamiliar situation which the author attempts to explore permit us to follow his arguments only in the mind."

The first moon burial was carried out on July 31, 1999. The cremains of Eugene Shoemaker, an expert in lunar geology and impact cratering as well as Father of the Science of Near-Earth Objects, were laid to rest when the Lunar Propector spacecraft, after eighteen months of circling the moon and obtaining data for the scientists back at NASA, was ordered to crash into the moon.

On earth, Shoemaker had convinced others that Arizona's Meteor Crater was caused by a rock from space, that we could be struck by what lay beyond the bounds of our atmosphere.

The year he died, Tsiolkovsky said, "I began to dream of possible voyages away from our planet when I was seventeen. In 1895, I wrote a [science fiction] book called *Speculations on Earth and Sky* ... I am now seventy-eight, but I still continue to calculate and invent an imaginary reactive machine. So much have I thought on it, so many thoughts have passed through my head. These are not fantasies...."

In 1972, the last man on the moon fell on his knees in the dust of the moon's surface, sending gray residuals on separate vectors, traveling at the same velocity. Rising, he considered how long the folds of his space suit would track the ground beneath him.

In 1958, the year before the Russian Luna 3 spacecraft sent down the first photographs of the far side of the moon, a rocket was built out of stone. Standing next to it, one arm held out, as if to brace the tall, thin craft, a figure of Tsiolkovsky stands on a stone block that marks the scientist's grave. Another rocket in relief crowns his carved words:

*In all probability, the better part of mankind will not succumb, but will move from sun to sun in search of fresh energy. After many decillions of years, we shall perhaps be living near a sun that has not yet begun to shine, but exists only in a primordial state, in the form of nebulous matter destined for higher things.*

# The Book of
# Concealed Hearts

F or a long time, I thought those were trees," said the
museum guard from behind me. Over the past two hours,
I had been wandering around an exhibit called *Picturing Eden* and
the stillness of the rooms provided the privacy I needed to
become so startled by his sudden interjection. I turned to him
then followed his gaze back to the darker photograph of trees in a
moss-covered forest. He brandished a small flashlight and
directed a beam of light over my shoulder and onto the trunks,
arresting a pair of glazed eyes. The trees were covered with animal
pelts: a large animal with small ears; it appeared to be a rodent
with a cone-like face pointed toward the sky. He extinguished the
light and the eyes faded, the forest receded and it was as though

we had just been in a northern woods, lush and designed like some tampered, luring world. Holstering his light, he looked down at me and said, "I bet people walk through these rooms for days and don't see that. Now you see."

As I walked through a bookstore this morning the woman behind the counter exclaimed to a regular customer just entering the store, "You have no hat!" It was five below outside. He said oh well he couldn't find it and she said how her toes froze and her face dried up on the walk to work and people should really stay inside in temps like these. And he said he hoped it would snow, that it's been snowing over by the lakes and locals are making a concerted effort to measure the depth of the daily falls by taking a plastic ruler to the picnic table. They make sure to wait until after the snow has had time to compact of its own accord and only then offer an accurate reading. The woman behind the counter said, "I've seen those people on TV, wrestling their red and black shovels up onto the roofs to get the snow down, to keep the ceilings from caving in. They've been falling for days."

My father writes from an undisclosed location on the east coast of America. We have not exchanged messages in years, not since my mother died and he sent me the article on the 2001 Maoist massacres in Nepal, with a handwritten note copied across the top: "FYI, thinking of you."

He says the birds in Texas are dying. They are falling in mid-flight to the ground, right downtown on Congress Avenue. Not just one or two, he says, but sixty or so and how is Hunter, his other daughter, with whom he urges me to make contact, as though she too might be falling.

And Hunter says the Great-Tailed Grackles and pigeons that follow them around did die but no one could really say for what reason. What concerns me, she says, is the flooding throughout the downtown area. The unrelenting rains she stays up all night listening to on the brown couch that has become ragged and must be thrown out and I say the gold one, the gold couch?

She says you know those people who get washed away down the river? They're not stupid people; you think that, you think, why in the world did they lob caution out the window and barrel into deep waters; but sometimes lakes look like puddles and by then it's too late and by then your engine fails and your tires are lifting, lifting, rising, and you're drifting in this box of steel, waving to the onlookers lining the shores like some queen on a float.

Hunter wants to know if I still think often of our mother and I say no, not really, because what I really think about is zero-gravity and whether or not I'm satisfied with the current state of my mattress or if it's time to trade the sagging thing in because we so often underestimate the amount of support required for comfort and she says she thinks about Deepak Chopra.

She wants to know if our mother is up there looking down on us and I say I don't think energy is so easily created or destroyed and Hunter thinks we get reincarnated. So I say our mother may be a giraffe. And she thinks our mother is a person.

"Like she's some other person, somewhere on earth?"

"Yea."

And I think of people in Times Square, walking.

He got on at Davenport, about an hour and a half from my arrival home. We were all bussing it across the Midwest, trying to make it home before the blizzard hit. The bus driver, in no hurry, was attempting the route for the first time and occasionally relied on me for directions. I said we must have missed the turn because there goes the John Deere Factory. He radioed in for help as we trundled on south. Then he turned to me and said there's nothing more you can do.

He got on at Davenport and he was wearing jeans and a denim jacket, just like my father used to wear and my mother would say, close enough for him to hear, "I see he's got his prison suit on again." I can't remember if he started wearing them before or after he began the affair. My instinct is to say after. We all want evidence of lost love, as though given adequate foresight we could avoid certain pains.

He was wearing denim and when he bent to place his duffel bag in the empty seat by the window before sitting down, the denim dipped to reveal an enormous divide. Thumbing through a yellow magazine with a picture of a handgun on the cover and the word COMBAT across the top, he snuck glances in my direction and pulled his earphones tight around his neck.

At the rest stop, he ordered a chicken sandwich and when the man at the register asked which he preferred, "baked or fried," he stuck his index finger in his mouth, leaned on one foot then the other and said he didn't know the difference.

He sat down to eat the baked chicken sandwich, unfurled the silver wrap and took two bites before throwing the rest away. I watched from the window looking out on the parking lot and gas pumps.

On his way back out to the bus he stopped to show me a picture of his sister, her husband, and their son, all of them blonde-headed. He said he was on his way to Des Moines and hoped we'd get there before the blizzard hit. Then he leaned in and said, "I did a bad thing. That's why they sent me to Phoenix." He had pulled a knife out in front of someone then delivered it into this someone's stomach. It happened quickly and then he was sent away. He said he was calmer. We stood by the window watching snow skitter across asphalt, too cold yet to adhere and accumulate.

Hunter says the woman down the street started looking for the dog by pulling out the kitchen drawers and placing each utensil on the counter. Days later she doused the lawn furniture in kerosene and stood over the plastic chairs with a lit match in her raised right fist. She hated the sound of the ice cream truck and her husband would periodically find bits of torn paper all over the house that read, "Kill the ice cream man!" When her husband called the authorities, she ran into the woods, hid beneath the brush. They searched for hours. Finally they found her, strapped her to the gurney and as they wheeled her away she said, "We're going for a ride."

An eight-lane bridge in the Midwest descends five stories to rest at the bottom of a river. "The best perspective we can provide is aerial," says a woman reporting from the field and follows with a question for a rescuer, "How would you describe the scene: pandemonium or chaos?" and a rescuer responds, "Chaotic but calm," and again she says, "How would you describe the scene?" and he says, "Scene of mourning," and she says, "How would you describe the sound?" and he turns to gaze down at the current wending around white cars with grills planted in silt, doors thrown wide and he says, "Several people are pinned or trapped, deceased," and adds that "Seventy to eighty thousand bridges in America are considered 'structurally impaired' or 'functionally obsolete' and this does not mean they are unnavigable."

"Tell me if you think this sounds suspicious," my sister says. A girl named M., a French major from L.A., a nice girl into current affairs, used to live across from my sister's apartment complex. M. said her neighbor was abusing his kids; M. heard constant screaming. So M. called the cops.

The neighbor found out and took revenge by squirting Elmer's glue in M.'s car door. M. moved. Then, "and this is the suspicious part," my sister adds, M. started hearing her new neighbor verbally abusing his girlfriend. "He screamed, she screamed. She seemed scared," said M. So M. called the cops.

"Don't you think that's a little suspicious, to happen two times," says my sister, searching for patterns. And I wonder if she's really asking: what's so strange about a love that sounds detrimental to people who are not involved?

Pollution may be seeding the atmosphere with particles around which water vapor gathers and forms clouds, which reflect the sun's light and heat back into space, and this deflection of light means the Earth's atmosphere has been cooling, by 1.8 degrees centigrade some scientists say and add that this lack of light and heat may mask the full effects of global warming, and that some places have ten percent less sunlight, like Israel, and other places have thirty percent less sunlight, like Russia, and they call this global dimming.

"We have yet to understand the incredible power of the mind," says my sister, and adds, "Jack Canfield, you know the guy who did those Chicken Soup books, well he's come to preach this thing called the Law of Attraction. He has a video out on it, called *The Secret*. He says you can get anything you want in your life by attracting it. You want to be happy, you say it out loud: 'I want to be happy.' You have to ask the universe, you have to open yourself up. You know what Jack would say about you, he would say you're sending out negative vibes and it's even being stated out loud. You need to say, 'I'm looking forward to starting over.' You need to say, 'I want to meet a guy.'" She says, "I tried it, I said, 'I want to meet a guy.' It was stupid; I think you have to be more specific, you have to associate positive feelings with it. For example, people always say, when it rains it pours...guys don't ask me out for weeks and then all of a sudden. You will get results in time. Jack says zero to six months."

She adds, "So are you going to watch the video, which normally costs $29.95 but is currently available for download at $4.95?"

I rode my bike in to town and as I was locking it up, a girl approached me, wobbled back and forth, then said, "I'm going to pass out." She lurched toward me, as though falling and I caught her, wrapped one thin arm around my neck and helped her to a nearby café. She sat down inside while someone brought her a glass of water. A crowd gathered around her. Then she looked up at the faces, as if seeing them for the first time and said, "I'm leaving." She stood up abruptly, tilted back and forth and huffed as though the earth itself were moving. Then she fell toward the exit, catching herself with each delayed step. At the door, she turned back to us as we stared on, confused. "Go ahead, laugh," she said then left.

My father writes to say he wants me to know that he is close to buying a house in the city where we were a family for twelve years long ago. He says it is large and ideal for a father and daughter to share, with space galore and that it has been a very long time since either of us has had a place we can call home. "I will be the only one living there so I hope u will consider your home as well. The entire third floor has two large rooms with a full bath and is separate from the rest of the house. I haven't closed on this deal yet but am trying hard." He is turning through empty rooms in downtown Richmond, Virginia framed by abandoned warehouses, newly erected museums of past devastation, and the two foot thick flood wall of the surrounds. I imagine him placing a twin bed here, the chest of drawers made of pine over there, a bookshelf, a rug; we will paint the walls yellow like the fresh sunflowers we will buy on Sundays and keep in the kitchen, he thinks, because they will make optimists of us.

Over the phone my grandfather calls me by my mother's name and after a while I stop correcting him because it is the ninth time and really what is the harm. Before hanging up he says, "Remember, we miss you, love you, and we know where you live."

# Crime Scene

About a mile down Fremont St., in Las Vegas, NV, a mile past the horse and rider rearing their flat neon frames into the steeling light, Stella floats face up in the motel pool. Her grey, oversized t-shirt clings to the three mounds of breast and belly that break the surface of the water. I sit in a metal rusted chair by the five-foot-deep end, press my fork into a plate of soggy pancakes, and watch the syrup bubble up between the prongs.

Stella says, *You know you can make a pretty decent living off of felling trees.* She tilts her head back to keep the water from her words. *Find some cheap land in Maine, let the trees grow all over it. And, in the fall, they bring a good chunk of change. You might want to think about getting some land up there.* I imagine evergreens sticking straight up from her breasts, straight like furled construction paper.

My mother liked to tell the story about my older sister's eighth grade history project. The assignment called for a model of the solar system. When the day came to hand over her design, my sister offered her No. 2 pencil like a lollipop. Impaled on the lead end was a piece of crumpled notebook paper at the center of which was written *world.*

\*

When my mother first asked me about life after death, I told her *people die.* She nodded at me, seated on her lap and considering the shadows beneath the arches of her Marilyn Monroe curls. I was twelve; she was forty-four. We were sitting in a plaid green chair in the living room. The television was off, the house quiet. She thought for a few seconds then asked, *So you don't think there's any sort of higher being?*

*No.*
*No one waiting on the other side?*
*No.*
*What about space?*
*What about it?*
*Don't you think there must be someone else out there?*
*Like aliens?*
*Well. . .*
*Maybe. But, where's the evidence.*
*So what you're saying is that we're just basically our bodies.*

*Pretty much. We get buried or cremated and recycle back into the earth. Uh huh.*

I mashed a curl between my thumb and forefinger and, rolling it, added, *I think cremation is better, you take up less room, and it probably speeds up the whole recycling thing anyway. I bet they'll be shipping our remains out on rockets pretty soon.*

★

Stella points beyond the roof of our motel, at a plane still stretching from the earth. *Look, the underside is all lit up.* Although the sun had set, its rays were still lipping past the horizon to glance the plane's underbelly: a warm yellow dot tracking the dark sky. I had been traveling haphazardly around the U.S., in a baby blue Ford I bought off an aging hippie-gone-stock broker four months ago in San Francisco. He had run to the corner of the street, watching as I steered away from the Mission District, the letters on the license plate becoming illegible with distance: ONAFLIT. Some sort of consolation really. When you live alongside a person who is dying, you make plans. At thirteen I began requesting maps from: 800-GOCALIF; 800-UTAH-FUN; 888-ENJOY-IN; 800-NATURAL; 800-2-CONNECT. I asked for California, Utah, Illinois, Arkansas, and Indiana—anything west of Virginia really. And when they arrived I took them quietly up to my room and unfolded them, making sure the seams did not tear. I taped them to the ceiling and fell asleep thinking of new ways west.

★

It occurs to me that I've been looking for a mother figure. And I want this to mean something. Like, *the people we love live on in details of strangers*, or, *a sorrow shared is half a sorrow*, or, *if I found enough heartbreaking moments they could reconstruct love before loss.*

★

People rarely question the motivation of clouds. As icons they are fluffy puffballs pulled apart to various degrees; as metaphors they are penises, donuts, swans; and as adjectives they are billowing, voluminous, mungo, scopic, sometimes cloyed.

But *nacreous clouds* sounds a bit more menacing; the prefix puts a person on edge. These are the seldom seen clouds of the stratosphere's uninhabitable heights. Most often observed at dawn or at dusk, when the sun's rays angle over the horizon to arrest their undersides these iridescent clouds have been known to tease holes in the ozone. The latest sighting prompted one meteorological officer to describe them as *reflecting like an airborne mother-of-pearl shell* - - - - - - - - - - - - - - - - - - - - - - - - - - - - - - - - - - - - - - - - - - - - - - - - - - - - - - - - - - - - - - - - - - - - - - - - - - - - *mother of pearl;* - - - - - - *mother tongue;* - - - - - - - *mother nature; mother* - - - - - - - - - - - - - - - - - - - - *-ship; mother* - - - - - - - - - - - - - - - - - - - - *country*

★

The evening before leaving New York City: the summer sun settles into blue as I watch from my apartment stoop. A neighbor from four floors up returns from ballet rehearsal and sits next to me. He says he was an orphan with a drunken father in Detroit before he moved to the city to model and dance in the eighties. He wears a magnet on his elbow because it facilitates circulation, increases oxygen in the blood and heals muscles faster. He has a magnetic bed and says people don't sleep horizontally in soft beds and that's how they can tell when you die—by where the blood flows.

He says, *You know a girl exploded in your apartment and lay like that for eight days in the heat wave. I said it smelled like a dead body, not knowing she was dead.* He tells me to lengthen my spine or I'll end up hunched over in old age like the woman walking slowly past us and he puts his hand on my lower back then grabs my hand and drags it sideways across his lower back so we look like two principles preparing to rise from the stairs and commit to our long-legged entrance. He says the thing he remembers most about the day they carried the body out was how one cop had stood on the step above us and stared up into the night.

★

*Look*, my mother whispered, pointing to a woman eating potato chips one by one. We were seated at an airport gate, waiting. I looked at the woman: long brown hair, white tennis shoes, eyes flitting about nervously as she munched. *Isn't that beautiful? The way her hand turns out 180 degrees after she puts each chip in her mouth.*

★

It is before noon in Nevada. I've sold the van and bought a plane ticket back to the place where my mother died eight years ago. I imagine that this time I'll be able to gain a more lasting resolution, by visiting her grave once more.

59

As we prepare for take-off, a loud noise can be heard repeating beneath us. One woman exclaims to no one in particular that it sounds like a dog, like a dog trapped down there and it could be a dog because they allow that kind of thing these days and no one smiles at her because maybe they are thinking about the dog and isn't that sick so the woman says well maybe it's the belt that carries the luggage up and wouldn't that be a shame.

Flying over Las Vegas, I watch the shadow of our plane track beige mountains that descend steeply into a body of water so dark it looks as though space has filled the earth and the mountains they are floating and it feels like we're receding from a world more uncertain than our form overhead.

# *Reality is Recognizing Resemblances in Those Things Without Us*

Posit the sphere and herein lies your personal property. Here lies your prehensile limb, your stippling pretenses. Of stars and galaxies, a clasp comes undone. And, failing to bend back against an opening, one develops a habit of constructing wanton parallels to track the restless, endless horizon. Our distance is illustrated by the nearness of horizontal lines, which, as they venture further from each other, resemble sky, foreground, frame.

As we conquer the space between us, our distance does not expand infinitely but posits absence like a weapon declined by profiles that seduce and destroy the object we outline. In a café, a boy leans his elbows on a coffee table and snaps a plastic knife in half while a yellow-haired girl looks on. Across the street, a window beyond which a welder bends beneath his iron mask. A white light occasionally and two confronting silhouettes become one: as proximity is our suspect, as crime is our perfection.

*Tell me the one again about the pirates and the gold*, I say. And he tells it like a fairy tale: Suppose we have three fears of freedom and an arbitrary terror of presidents. One president will start off by proposing a way to divide the terror of freedom. If more than half the presidents reject the proposal, the first president is hijacked and another president steps up to begin the process anew. Presidents, apparently, love freedom and like seeing other presidents hijacked. They do not like being hijacked themselves.

The earth's surface is not a curve but an accumulation of straight lines laid side by side so near they resemble a turning. Raining for days and the river moves as though fast-forwarding in an otherwise still environment. Two men gaze downstream at a woman posing questions to a pair of swans, who turn away. The sodden ground gives way beneath our feet, delivering our bodies down in slight increments revealed by our shifting, correcting for posture, gravity, self-evident truths.

One is taken to know one. One is seared inside. One is potential realized in fear. One is a traction dull. One is a terrible thing to waste. One is Jesus' crisis. One is the fodder of leavened reason. One is a farther figure. Horses, many, the same color.

Discontent frequently resides in impairment of the subtle husband. Thermodynamics with a rising intonation. The diaphragm knows one motion only. To exhibit elements of an extraordinary and foreign shudder.

Suffering makes one the same person. I'll be solid ground; you be top of the world. I'll be down to earth; you be rising above. You be rising up. You be fine brindled blades with rulers. Loosing the line made sweet edge of sphere, she made a motion for stretching and her arm extended. One plum thumbnail against bare winter branches. One spring brought by reaching.

Hyperboles happen in happiness and horror, in sickness and in stealth. People say true dreams come but true love depends on optics. If a mark is significantly longer than it is wide, then a line has been drawn. If two lines converge on a plane, then a vanishing appears in one's future.

When a head shot of a poster child for *Virginity Rules* dissolves into a head shot of a wrestler accused of testosterone doping dissolves into a shot of an opera singer not ready for her role a shot of a grave to a shot of the hairiest man in China bidding to relay the torch a man claiming to be the sailor kissing the woman at end of the war a man has just left a mine collapsed on six workers, what must one think? Says the voiceover for a sleep aid to no one in particular, *Your dreams miss you.*

When we can no longer bear this solder-less self-tapping, we begin to collect information on the expiring mother—record of voice in slumber, record of face in laughter, the way mother figure bends, mother figure rises, folds bangs from forehead. We do this to protect against the sudden cessation of electricity, the bifurcation of the end bell, the spring-steel defects. This is not uncommon practice with respect to load-center, weatherproof socket. We require this warm resistor, threads field-winding inside the inductor.

# Land Without Land
# Is Not Land

He stares back with a laconic look, the lift of his eyebrows attempting to overcome the slumped torso and tired eyelids, as he sits on a sofa and glances over his shoulder in response to my mother who must have been holding the camera. I don't recognize the expression on his face and can't help thinking there must be some indication of the man who was trying to have both our family and another he could love. In the only other photograph I have of my father taken during this trip to the Chesapeake, his elbows are held out awkwardly to accommodate the hands which fumble to unwrap a block of cheese. His fingers and forearms seem gigantic and therefore apart from his body. If the hand is a site at which one encounters another then his suggest there's no world to which he might attend.

An eighteen-wheeler passes by carrying blades for the broken wind turbines at Horse Hollow Wind Energy Center, the world's largest wind farm. Hunter and I are driving west across Texas, passing by taxidermy shops, and peaches under roadside awnings. We're heading to McDonald Observatory in the Fort Davis Mountains and as we leave the sycamore, cyprus, and juniper trees of east Texas for the desert candles and creosote bush scrub of the west, highway signs warn of dangerous crosswinds. Hunter has her eyes closed. Then she opens them wide and when I ask why she says she saw a buzzard flying slowly across our windshield and it must have passed because she didn't feel anything.

With no trails or clearing, the land on either side of us, while near, appears untouched by humans, like some possible world by which we'd only pass. Expanding through the fields, light obfuscates the space between those things enclosed to be seen. *Ganzfeld* refers to a homogeneous surface from which no objects can be drawn forth. In 1930 Gestalt psychologist Wolfgang Metzger found that a brightly lit plaster wall quickly lost the attention of his subjects while the same wall dimly lit caused them to report seeing a fog, a mist of light; in other words, the perception of space with no evident limit: sight as an object apart from the self. Prolonged in this state, without continuous, changing input, the beholder occasionally experiences apparent blindness; the eye lacking purchase sees only black.

Exiting onto a deserted one-lane ranch road police lights appear in the rearview mirror. Without the siren we are so accustomed to hearing in advance of the car and its lights, the scene seems unreal. A sense of drama and immediacy set apart by distance. Then the sound rushes in, high-pitched. We watch the state trooper expand in the mirror then grow smaller as the car speeds toward the horizon and drops beyond view. Besides the direction this road provides, there's no indication of the reason for its brief appearance. Absence almost makes one believe such space couldn't help but give form to that which remains beyond apprehension.

We pass a fawn looking like a wing nut with its head stuck up out of the brush. At the station in Ozona, a man crouches next to a red gas can of change and points to his right where a white dog, black cat, and a black and white mouse lay stacked on one another according to size. Inside, our water and pretzels ring to $6.66 which Hunter claims is bad luck and throws gum on the counter. As the cashier scans the item he says we should know better than to mention the devil. A vase of drooping carnations sits on the counter.

Persistence is not the absence of change but a change so slow as to be imperceptible, inviting vigilance from the one who finds himself in an environment so vast it quickly becomes the imagined extension of his more immediate surrounds. Back on the road, Hunter sees a horse on its side in a field and says a horse on its side on the ground is dead.

"We feel we are at the bottom of this ocean of air;" writes James Turrell, "we are actually on a planet." Turrell, whose work centers primarily around light, reminds us that light is the medium by and through which we see ourselves seeing. In 1968, Turrell was invited, by fellow Light and Space artist Robert Irwin, to participate in the *Art and Technology* exhibit held three years later at the Los Angeles County Museum of Art. The project paired artists with scientists working in advanced technology. Turrell and Irwin joined psychologist Edward Wortz of the Garrett Aerospace Corporation in L.A. Dr. Wortz was exploring the perceptual experiences of astronauts in outer space at the time. The three soon began experimenting with Ganzfelds. Then, in July 1969, a few weeks after U.S. astronauts first landed on the moon, Turrell, offering little explanation to Irwin, withdrew from the experiments. He later wrote: "We have spent billions to go to the moon—we go to this lesser satellite called the moon and say we are in space, but we are in space right now; we just don't feel ourselves to be in space."

A vulture circles overhead. To look across this landscape is to witness the degradation of sight, as the eye finding nothing by which to locate the body, recedes before its potential undoing. While black vultures rely mainly on sight to track prey, turkey vultures have an unusually keen sense of smell, which distinguishes them from the Old World vultures descended from hawks and eagles. The use of this developed sense causes them to fly nearer the ground in search of day old carrion. If a leak is expected in a gas line, some companies will pump ethyl mercaptan, a chemical that smells like the gas emitted by the decomposition of a body, through the pipeline and watch to see where the turkey vultures gather. Both black and turkey vultures may be considered social foragers, aware of their kettle spread across the sky like a net.

Nothing rises out here except the occasional spire or tower against the horizon; or, the dust the wind turns up in narrow columns Hunter attempts to point out before each dissipates. We pick up only one station on the radio and Hunter is sick of country. She sighs, turns the radio off, suffers the silence for a few minutes then says she shot a gun at a range and wouldn't like to go hunting unless we were hunting birds because she could shoot a bird or she could shoot at a bird since she'd surely miss or take a feather from a wing and while not sure she could shoot a horse it may be very easy to shoot a horse.

With no air, there is no speech or light and we fail to gain a

74

sense of either the limitlessness of space or the presence of a boundary. At the edge of the Painted Desert in northern Arizona, Turrell's epic *Roden Crater* shapes the perception of space by ground, presenting light as the mark seen through to draw forth some structure beyond us. Lying in the earthwork with one's head pointed down toward its center, it's said the observer sees space enclosed by the rim of the crater, a portion of sky viewed without reference to horizon so it appears to descend. Many critics have likened the crater to an eye, the organ, says Turrell, as a site at which the mind is most vulnerable.

Following our parents' separation Hunter cut off all contact with our father. It was probably the more sensible decision. When this happened, he adopted a black cat and named her Beatrice; opened an antique booth and called it Willow Place. He loved tramp art and brought home a thre- foot-wide cedar clock tower that lit up when plugged in. I wanted to stay in touch but he often forgot we had plans, forgot birthdays, sometimes wouldn't call or write for six months or more at a time. He said there was a room for me in his house but he often left near the bed a dildo, lubricant, and handcuffs. He lived with a roommate who was overly kind, had difficulty concentrating, would move through the house. When they fought he would call to ask if I didn't think my father loved him.

Our mother kept a clipboard by her bed. Attached was a newspaper article that listed the characteristics of a sociopath. "There's a name for people like your father," she'd say, gesturing with the clipboard. It was the same way she would periodically mumble, as if testing my reaction, "No child wants to see her father in prison." He'd used her money to take his lover to New England, the Chesapeake, Anguilla, Paris, Rome, and Florence. She hired a detective to retrace their travels. Embezzlement was easier to substantiate than the intention behind his calls to the hospital where she was having a breast removed. He wanted to help her, he'd say, he missed her, hadn't done anything wrong, it was all in her head, he could forgive her. Her mother had died of lung cancer when she was thirteen. She imagined us watching her. Sometimes she had the thought her body, cut to be rid of certain cells, might make her appear more desirous to him.

"[T]here never is no light," says Turrell. "Even when all the light is gone, you can still sense light."

Hunter spots the blinking lights of a helicopter and says it looks like it's on its way to the hospital in San Angelo where Adam works. Since they started dating a year ago, she has become increasingly aware of flight patterns in the area. She says, in a helicopter, if it's windy you feel the wind. And there's no air-pressure system, no radar, one engine, one bolt called "the Jesus" to hold down the blades.

Helicopters hit birds all the time and large birds break through windows. "If it breaks through windows wouldn't it also break through shields?" I ask. And has he hit birds before, is it a common occurrence? A common occurrence, she says, is a telephone line that tangles and turns you upside down. A common occurrence is losing the Jesus. Do you get electrocuted? No, she says, it's more about getting turned over. You can hear the patient through your helmet and the medics in the back and sometimes they can hear you talking with the tower.

Hunter agreed to go on a flight a few months ago. On the drive to the hospital, however, she crested a hill and found the truck in her lane had been hit; another was on its side in a ditch while a green car lay in between. She was first on the scene, says it seemed the accident happened because the trucks were trying to avoid the car. You've got to leave your vehicle when the helicopter comes and Adam lands right in front of her. He's not allowed to get out of the helicopter because it's all about speed. She imagines him looking back through the shield attached to his helmet, imagines herself as the patient then medic. He's advised to stare straight ahead so he doesn't get emotionally involved. He has to fly a different direction depending on how a body is injured. If you get burned you go to Dallas. If you get crushed you go to Abilene.

# Feng Shui

I passed a gaggle of two-foot-tall children standing next to a minivan with the long side door slid back they resembled penguins in big coats that buoyed their arms a woman rounded the van looked down at them and said what were you all born in a barn close the door uncertain really of what to do next they teetered back and forth flapping their arms against their sides then one said to the other hey joe were you born were you born in a barn.

My sister says shes reading about feng shui and that you are supposed to clear your entry way and did I remember that table in front of the door to her apartment as you entered and she says she moved it.

.   .   .

So the qi can flow freely into the home and I tell her about the men who flew balloons to the stratosphere to the place that is uninhabitable and cold and the men would pass out from hypoxia and begin to descend and reawaken but sometimes they would not or sometimes it would be too late.

And she says mirrors should not reflect a wall because the qi gets trapped there back and forth running up against the wall up against the mirror and she adds you know if youre married in the bedroom youre not supposed to put your bed directly below a ceiling beam because it creates a subconscious divide between you and your partner as though the beam were running between you.

Not up there but right between you and I say they went on like that for years rising losing descending and she says why dont we go to that balloon festival in new mexico next year.

# *Without You the World Is Complete*

Raptors are not social beings; they are not pining for one's presence; one's touch is not a positive thing. Nor do pairs pass time together unless tending a nest at that moment; while certain gestures and sounds made unwittingly perhaps will be noticed and turned over by the dog who finds meaning, the raptor will do no such thing. Living in the plane where ocean and sky are shifting, conterminal, a falcon sees nine times that of the farthest-sighted man and nothing rises out of what is not already known. Broomcorn is grown to make brooms; willows, baskets. Wine bowls take up wine while cornhusks are twisted to weave mats or make dolls. Ravens, crow-like, but with wedge-shaped tails. One writes a history of the world in moonlight and tragically the universe is fond of those clouds that refuse. While three dots eventually trace the body from a head, accumulation may signal disease. If the heart breaking illuminates all other pain in the body when does the heart stop breaking?

Some delight in throwing a shield against armor. The ear seeks out a break in sound; a break in sight seeks the eyes. While water may act as a magnifier, the beheld often lacks definition. Having piloted his submersible through the depths of an ocean, explorer William Beebe wrote, *The hundreds of nets I have drawn through the sea offered only a harvest which served to enhance this desire to descend.* When moisture in a cloud increases from 12 to 3000 microns in diameter, a *droplet* becomes a *raindrop* and falls. If the heart beats though the lamb does not breathe, hold its hind legs and swing it in circles. The end conforms to an internal order in which one appears to shudder. Grain will shimmer, eyes swell. No matter, a series of profiles. Bear the body out on a ship of flames at sunset.

Erosion shapes an arch by rock fall and wind while a natural bridge is formed from the river that passes below. Hollow cutting is tracing the shadow that lies between a candle and paper soon cut and backed with black. Once the device for measurement is created, it remains forever subject to refinement. Refined rod puppets, used in the Javanese theatre of "wayang golek," are depicted with narrow features, bowed heads, their movements are slow, smooth, their voices are soft, scrutinized as though any slight dispersal may be magnified in meaning detrimental when confronted by myriad interpretations. While "wayang" means "shadow" or "ghost" one may also read "puppet" or "performance."

Before a life-size photograph titled "Octopus," a man with a stroller says to the child, "See that? That's a squid. Calimari." But in pointing to the subject, he looks over at the woman looking on across the room. A silhouette telegraphs meaning made with the hands and cannot be grasped until the body turns about it. On the back of his *Complex Presentiment (Half-Figure in Yellow Shirt)*, Kasimir Malevich wrote, *The composition coalesced out of elements of the sensation of emptiness, of loneliness, of the exitlessness [besvykhodnosti] of life.* Cloud bases appear pink over desert sands and dilation shifts perspective. One oceanographer, to describe the effect of a force of air across a body of water, coined the term *wind-driven gyres.* An eye is not the shape of a mouth; a body, not a stage before pain.

# Karman Vortex

*Often they don't let go of the musical instrument even in water.*
—Gian Francesco Bracciolini

Wingless planes were created to test the concept of flying a body back from space, to a predetermined site on Earth's surface, by using the force of aerodynamic lift. First and foremost they are bodies, not ballistics. While ballistic reentry relies solely on drag to slow a craft through its descent, the lifting reentry uses the force generated from the deflection of air away from a body. Some scientists called it *style*, as in: "Don't be Rescued from Outer Space—Fly Back in Style." With swollen undersides and blunt noses shaped to hold a heated shock-layer at safe distance, these are the planes that do not aspire to their more apparently beautiful Air Force X-series counterparts. At the time, their designers considered them a likeness in which the Space Shuttle might be built. They called them "lifting bodies." They are lifting because, above all, an astronaut is a pilot; and they are lifting, in the late 1950s, because engineers hoped these crafts might reenter the atmosphere and return a pilot to a runway rather than an ocean.

The first lifting body was a glider made of wood and pulled into the air over Rogers Dry Lake with the help of a 1963 Pontiac Catalina. This car featured a new design including squared-off bodylines, cruise control, AM/FM radio, and a steering wheel capable of being tilted to any one of six different angles. This Catalina, based on the model that won the Bonneville Salt Flats time trials in Utah the year before, was capable of towing the thousand pound M2-F1 one hundred and ten miles per hour in under thirty seconds. On March 1, 1963, the M2-F1, "M" for manned and "F" for flight, carried its wheels up from the ground and was soon after named the "Flying Bathtub." By the end of April, it had flown forty eight times. Having proven itself under these basic conditions, the model was escorted north to the NASA Ames Research Center in Northern California where it was mounted on three twenty-foot-tall struts in order to test how well it might withstand a bank of electric-powered fans generating a 135 mile per hour "wind."

It was here that engineers noticed the presence of a "Karman vortex." In 1911, engineer and aerodynamicist Theodore von Karman found that the air which turns behind a body takes the shape of a vortex. It was a theory made popular when he later applied it to an investigation surrounding the collapse of the Tacoma Narrows Bridge. Built as an alternative to taking a boat from a city to a peninsula, this bridge was the first to turn itself in pieces and plunge into the waters of the Sound. It was called "the most beautiful bridge in the world." And to convince others that this slender span might withstand a force of nature, its lead engineer developed the theory of deflection, which claimed "dead weight" might provide the strength necessary to uphold the lateral force of wind. Although one edge waved as much as twenty eight feet higher than the other just before its collapse on November 7, 1940, the Governor of Washington initially claimed no fault in the design and announced a plan to rebuild the structure. On reading of the disaster, von Karman wrote in from Pasadena, urging the state to reconsider; and he followed the request by likening this instability to that of a poorly made wing. A month later the Federal government invited him to participate in an investigation. Von Karman agreed and, on arriving at the meeting, said, *I represent the wind*.

The more curved a wing the more drag it generates; the less curved, the less drag and less lift. The faster the wing moves through the air, the more lift it produces—so long as the wing does not stall. The wing stalls when the airflow breaks into turbulent eddies; turbulence results in more drag and less lift. The wing stalls when the angle of attack is severe; the angle of attack is the degree at which a wing meets airflow; this is the incline that allows a craft to depart from the ground at low-speeds. A voice begins with the thought that must be set apart from a body.

"[They] couldn't see how a science applied to a small unstable thing like a wing could also be applied to a non-flying structure," von Karman said of the engineers involved in the Narrows investigation. When he first heard of the collapse, von Karman had been working on a model of a supersonic wind tunnel, a structure which must withstand a wind speed of up to Mach 5. A few years later he would design the army's first large supersonic tunnel at Aberdeen Proving Ground in Maryland—the first of its kind to be used for practical testing of supersonic bodies. By 1949, at least three supersonic wind tunnels were planned for construction in response to support from the newly established National Unitary Wind Tunnel Plan Act.

The wind tunnel is an invention derived from a "whirling arm." Eighteenth century English mathematician Benjamin Robins was the first to employ this device. At a length of four feet, the arm spun around in a circle, reentering its wake and drawing attention to the force that keeps an object from moving freely through the air. A few years later, Sir George Cayley, Father of Aviation, built a five-foot-long arm that spun at a rate nearly ten times that of his contemporary. Cayley is credited with many inventions including self-righting life-boats, tension-spoke wheels, caterpillar tractors, automatic signals for railway crossings, seat belts, and the first successful heavier-than-air vehicle: the monoplane glider. Drawing on data from his whirling arm, he discovered the four forces of flight—weight, drag, thrust, lift—and found that it is not the motion of the wing that provides lift but the movement of air around it. As a result, he rejected the feasibility of the *ornithopter*, a device that relied on the popular belief that humans could fly like birds by flapping their arms.

A bridge too will fly. And to prove his point, von Karman insisted on testing the new model for the Tacoma Narrows in a wind tunnel. As a result of his experiments, many were convinced that a bridge, like a wing, might lift. His was a theory later used to explore other phenomena as well, including the musical tones of the Aeolian harp and the problem of the "singing propeller." In the case of the latter, a high tone is emitted from the device responsible for moving a craft through the depths of an ocean; it is a sound capable of drawing another near.

# The Body

I sat in the chair opposite my mother who was busy feeding strands of red, brown, and green yarn into the pattern for a sweater with the design of a tree knitted over the chest. When she saw me she dropped the work and scowled. "What do you think you're doing?" she asked then, looking down as if suddenly realizing the knitting needles in her hands, answered her own question, "You're sitting on Sophie." Over the past few months my mother had grown increasingly wary of my presence. She began talking with an imaginary person she called Sophie. I would watch my mother's side of the exchange from the doorway of her bedroom. Sometimes Sophie made her smile or blush as she threw her head back in laughter. Other times, my mother appeared inert, hands poised in the air as if preparing to cross between two worlds—the one where we existed and the one to which Sophie belonged. I tried to convince her once of the illusion by moving my arms through the space to demonstrate, "There is no Sophie." I wanted to pull her back into the world. "You're cruel," she said. But by that point she'd made no attempt to rescue Sophie. In fact, she seemed to have let the matter go completely.

Through the snow that covers the river's frozen surface a single track of footprints bends from one shore to the other. I scan the line, searching for some alter in stride, anything to suggest a question, hesitation, doubt. I've heard Inuit fishermen would tell stories of those who paddled out in their kayaks, alone, certain at first of their orientation: charting by sun, horizon, the confidence of one's inexplicable relationship with a home environment. But because of the lack of contrast in the snow-filled landscape, combined with the rhythm of paddling the kayak, these men had been known to lapse into a hypnotic state and keep paddling until they had wandered far out to sea without hope of return. I imagine it a sort-of bewitching, imagine something else was involved: the vision of a past love, a proffered faith. I try to convince myself that self does not lead self to death.

Staring down at a field of unbroken snow I watch as the expanse appears to contract around two foci, as though presenting its action to the mechanism of the eye itself. We will tend to trust the sound of certain words in meaning's stead. Some etymologists have attempted to trace the word blizzard to the French *blesser* "to wound." Others have tried to make a connection with the German *blitz* for "lightning." There are owls capable of diving eighteen inches into a bank of snow to capture prey. This snow-plunging can be detected from wing prints left on a surface.

. . .

On March 7, 1874, sudden winds and overwhelming draughts of snow caused a reporter for the *Northern Vindicator*, an Estherville, Iowa, newspaper largely credited with originating the word *blizzard*, to write: "It is none of your one-horse snow-storms, but a regular old fashioned blizzard one of those in which people, in going to their woodpiles or stables, tie clothes lines to their door knobs, and pull themselves home." While Robley Dunglisons' 1829 list of Americanisms considered *blizzard* "a violent blow," and Davy Crockett, in his autobiography, five years later, used the word to refer to "a rifle shot," here is a blizzard like a labyrinth.

"My doubts stand in a circle around every word," wrote Kafka, "I see them before I see the word...." I imagine the *Vindicator's* qualifications of "regular" and "old fashioned" reveal a wish to reinforce one's experience of the world over the way language creates categories that sort and reclaim these experiences—that a word might stand in for a body by determining what we think.

Walking along the river I was thinking about Sophie when I noticed large sheets of ice jostle border ice in passing; a sign of upstream breakups brought on by the recent shock of warm weather. Flakes crinkled in accumulation: a hollow sound gathering. It seems each name, by determining a form, is an attempt to fix time—anchor, bullet, candle, crystal, frazil slush, freezups, grease, honeycomb, pancake, plate.

When my mother first presented Sophie, I had been afraid the figment, in drawing me away from a reasonable sense of the word, would draw me toward some vague, unwitting demise. As I watched my mother's mind piece and her body rot, I began to think death a gradual sloughing off of the functions which place the body in a world. It was a process I thought, well-contemplated, might slow, as though by simply witnessing one could suspend the act.

At night I snuck past my mother's room and out the front door, pushed the old sedan out of the driveway and down the street until it reached a speed at which I could hop in and pop the clutch into gear. If my mother could picture where I was—the Byrd Theatre down on Cary Street, the coffee shop across from Buddy's, Belle Isle where the Confederates once kept their Yankees captive on a strip of land in the middle of the James River—then I pictured her in pain. And I calculated how much blood a person could lose in the time I was gone.

Sometimes I drove to the run-down neighborhoods where my father lived. Former tobacco warehouses flanked one side of the downtown floodwall. I imagined being up there, surrounded by so many panes of glass, the horizon parted in squares capable of being rearranged; for instance, how the sky framed could be placed at ground level.

More often I went to the late night coffee shop where Wyatt liked to play chess. Wyatt had pale blue eyes and a habit of pausing for what seemed a long time before speaking. We rode out on his motorcycle, to the country, to get away, he said, from the artificial light. I let the palms of my hands hover against his shirt, just touching the soft area above his hips and below his ribs.

Still giddy from the night, I snuck back home around 5:30 in the morning, tiptoed upstairs to my room and pulled the covers over. Ten minutes later my mother opened the door, hand at her chest, heaving, and fell to the floor. I started toward her but she raised a palm to indicate I had no place. We stared at each other. "Look at me," she said then left.

．　．　．

One day during the spring of my senior year in high school my mother called and asked that I come home. When I got home I found her stuffing our dishrags, red though no longer plaid, into the hole in her chest. She had been hemorrhaging and looked down at the soft tissue as though inviting us to blame the wound instead of her. To avoid disturbing the clots she hoped had formed, we peeled the fabric back slowly and allowed it to fall, bunching at our feet. She handed me a clean white gown with the words GO AWAY centered across the front. I gathered it up to the neck then placed it over her head, helping her work the swollen left arm through. When lifted, though, this arm stretched the flesh open and a rank smell emerged.

She didn't want to go back to the hospital because she was afraid they wouldn't let her leave. She wanted to die at home, in her bed. She ran her right hand over her head; was it alright to go out in public without a wig? I put an arm around her waist and held her hip against mine to walk to the car.

It was probably a mistake to take the old Honda I'd gotten for my sixteenth birthday. The car was a stick shift and I was still, as my mother would describe it, "herky-jerky" behind the wheel. At the time, she had insisted on giving me my first lesson, as if to inaugurate this point in her youngest daughter's life. And though she'd threatened by the end of the driveway to get out and walk home if I didn't quit the herky-jerky, she'd managed to stay in the car, theatrically braced between window and dash, for one loop around the neighborhood.

In the car she hunched over and gave me that look again. On the way to the hospital, she accused me of overemphasizing stops, stripping the gears, seeking out rugged alterations in the road.

And she punctuated this measure with occasional shrieks pulled back into her mouth once noticed.

I see my mother propped up in the hospital bed; she looks at me with a horrified expression, "Who are you? What are you doing here?" It's a few hours past midnight. She glances hurriedly around the room for a place to put me. "You have to hide!" Her eyes are open unusually wide. She doesn't recognize that I'm her daughter. She tells me to lean back in the chair as though a body could blend into oblivion by approximating this recline. Then she pouts, crosses her arms and attempts to contort her body so I fall outside her field of vision. When she turns back, she is attempting to cry as she asks me to crouch down in the corner of the room behind the hospital bed. Better yet, climb into the poster of hot air balloons rising over a lake in which they are reflected. She says she'll tell me when it's safe to come out.

When she starts thrashing, I can see the catheter in her jugular vein pushing out against the skin of her neck. "You got us in this," she says, "you get us out." I reach for the nurse call button but she finds it first. I dig her fingers from the button before pressing it a couple times for good measure. She thinks I'm calling people who will come to kill us.

In a few minutes, a nurse will arrive and calm her. And the confusion will be explained as a transient ischemic attack, a small stroke. But my mother will, pointing without looking at me, keep insisting, "I don't know who *she* is."

# *Dear Sound of Footstep,*
# *Move Me or Tread.*

*If We Likened the Universe to a Shape Most People Would Insist on a Circle. The Planes are Not Departing; His Words are Not a Sea; the Horizon, Not a Line that Shimmers. Out of Sight, You are All Things to Me, You are Everything to Me, Without You, Etc. Some Will Maintain the Oars of Our Love Prove First Among Ruin. Apple Ripened, If Not Reached. The Shape of a Heart Assumes the Color Red. Causality : Casualty. A Trigger is Not a Comma; a Hammer is Not a Hyphen; a Barrel is Not a Pause Suspended. The Most Provocative Touch is the One of Which You are Most Uncertain. Lines that Extend from a Circle and Share a Common End Resemble a Megaphone.*

## *If We Likened the Universe to a Shape Most People Would Insist on a Circle.*

Early viewers of panoramas remarked on the life-like rendering of nature in a depicted environment. They were amazed that such enclosures could inspire this feeling of expansion. They would turn, spin, disorient, and descend in pursuit of the tale around them. At times it seemed the birds were soaring soldiers falling and we remained still. *The aphorism is a form of eternity*, said Nietzsche. It derives from *apo* for beyond and *horizein* for boundary. In other words, nature was defined by that which an individual could not gather at once beneath his gaze. If you stand in front of me and we stand before a mirror, am I not the curve that begins at your edge?

### The Planes are Not Departing; His Words are Not a Sea; the Horizon, Not a Line that Shimmers.

Early panoramas were created by joining the seams of eight paintings and pushing the planes back. This bend approximates a circle, or, a simulation.

This bend creates A VIEWPOINT FOR EVERY POINT OF VIEW!

This bend embodies a distortion: one continuous, encompassing experience.

On visiting the Atlanta Panorama in 1939, Clark Gable said, *This is beautiful but one thing is missing.* A plaster-of-Paris mannequin, created in his likeness, lies dying in the bushes, a smile affixed to his face. Hegel once claimed to become aware of a limit is to simultaneously overcome and pass beyond. The horizon is the point at which distance determines the location of the unknown. In his *Italian Journey*, Goethe would write while crossing the Mediterranean: *No one who has never seen himself surrounded on all sides by nothing but the sea can have a true conception of the world and his own relation to it.* It is not the first mark on a page that destroys the illusion that the field could be otherwise. It is the first glimpse that conceives space in terms of the individual's limited ability to perceive. Even the slight shadow of an urn resembles a line rather than your ever-impending presence.

97

## *Out of Sight, You are All Things to Me, You are Everything to Me, Without You, Etc.*

The fastest man on earth tested safety belts, ejection seats, and the limits of human deceleration. The *Gee Whiz* was a 680kg carriage secured by four *slippers* to a 610m track in New Mexico in 1947. The fastest man traveled faster on a rocket-sled than a .45-caliber bullet released from a single action. Occasionally the blood would rush into his eyes, causing him to see only red. Occasionally the blood would rush to the back of his head, causing him to see only white. A pool of water stood at the far end of the rocket-sled track to help arrest the fastest man. In the desert, bodies of water attract all kinds of life, including blackbirds and magpies. The red epaulets of a Red-Winged Blackbird determine its success in mating and in holding ground. At speeds above 600mph, the collision of man and bird would leave a life-like imprint in the man's breast. A coat of arms is formally described by the blazon that begins with the background, the shield. The fastest man's sight began to fade the day after his fastest run. The silhouette of a rocket plane remained seared into the retina of his right eye so that he may turn and place the plane against a body, before a mountain, above the sea.

## *Some Will Maintain the Oars of Our Love Prove First Among Ruin.*

In 1947, Yves Klein, the *artist of space*, began his monochrome paintings. He considered the monochrome an *open window to freedom, the possibility of being immersed in the immeasurable.* He thought blue a vital element in the color of infinity and with the help of a chemist he patented International Klein Blue (IKB). Blue, he said, *recalls the sea and the sky which are the most abstract aspects of tangible and visible nature.* He dipped nude women in IKB, directed them across a canvas, and called them *living brushes.* With a canvas strapped to the roof of his car, he drove seventy miles per hour in the rain, and called these *recordings.* In Paris, he sold empty space for gold, which he threw in the Seine and called this *restoring the natural order.* In *The Silent Art,* critic Lucy Lippard writes, *There is nothing lifelike about monotonal paintings,* and quotes Malevich, who said, *I have broken the blue boundary and come out into white.*

### Apple Ripened, If Not Reached.

The men who flew balloons to the stratosphere took color swatches to describe the blue of earth's edge. Color swatches are created by mixing pigments found on earth. He would sit in an aluminum chair by the fenced-in horses, close his eyes and have his hair cut. The first men who saw the curvature of earth from the height of a balloon described it as a *lifeless world*. Early descriptions of the stratosphere devolved into metaphors of unheard music, sight as feeling. As in: *I have the feeling that I should be able to see stars in this darkness but I can't find them.* The white background is ideal, limitless and otherworldly, until first sight. Of Kasimir Malevich's pioneering *White on White*, Klein claimed the artist was more concerned with the square than the color and added: *Malevich was actually standing before the infinite—I am in it.* A painting is not a window; a window is not a wall; a wall is not a line before longing. Denouncing NASA's trips to the moon, Klein documented his own lunar travel by picturing himself in black and white, angled in the air, arms stretched out over the line where sidewalk and street meet below, and he called this *Saut dans le vide (Leap into the Void)*.

## *The Shape of a Heart Assumes the Color Red*

A self-portrait was the first miniature painted by an American. Made in 1758, the image of Benjamin West was given, along with a marriage proposal, to Miss Elizabeth Steele, who took the likeness and declined the man. Tenderness cannot be exhibited in a place of no intention and time is not created from the details drawn forth by contemplation if not by sight. One does not exist to be verified by sense and slowing the approach of a touch does nothing to resolve the unavoidable violence staged to one's chagrin. Flooded with stimuli some falcons will develop a deep seated, unpredictable fear while those kept hooded and slowly allowed to see more light over time can be flown with less fear of loss. Miniature portraits insist the beholder project the idea of the one depicted into another world, an imagined world; some pleasing, private fathom of hereafter. In a tree, even the flutter of ochre leaves assumes discretion, as though neither the wind may be anticipated. Because these brushstrokes are so small, we are required to bend at the neck, to bow the head, so it appears we are praying or performing an act of devotion. Vision is an end in sight.

## Causality : Casualty.

The first trigger was employed in a single action. The single action was considered the shortest, lightest, smoothest pull. After each pull, the device must be prepared for the next round. The Cowboy, the Shooter, the Peacemaker and the Frontier, are examples of single actions. The sear retains the hammer until the trigger has received a certain force. The hammer springs and strikes a pin, in turn, which discharges a round. To follow a curved path, a body must undergo acceleration. Acceleration draws momentum from an accumulation of previous states in order to reach the next. *Weapon focus* refers to the inordinate amount of attention a witness will place on the device. If you hesitate before a field of lightning rods you are skewered and rising and we call you Eva Destruction. If the outcome of an event has not been observed, it exists in all possible states at once. Believe me when I say, *one must remain hidden in order to maintain the feeling that one sees completely*.

### *A Trigger is not a Comma; a Hammer is not a Hyphen; a Barrel is not a Pause Suspended.*

Of his *Uncertainty Principle*, Heisenberg said, *The more precisely the position is determined, the less precisely momentum is known in this instant.* The plow shape grip of a single action allows the device to rock back in the hand. This shape facilitates connection between thumb and hammer: preparation for the next pull. We could say no one is certain of both where one is and where one continues. An investigation is an act of creation. In his *On Certainty*, published posthumously, Wittgenstein writes, *For may it not happen that I* imagine *myself to* know *something?* Adultery has been known as both *crime against marriage* and *criminal conversation*. The patient says to the nurse suspending her breasts before him as she leans to read his blood pressure, *I see the light is on; please turn it off so I can sleep.*

### The Most Provocative Touch is the One of Which You are Most Uncertain.

This sentence contains four instances of the letter a,

one of m,

ten of n,

four of r,

and seven of s.

Rising through the upper atmosphere, one is often accompanied by feelings of freedom, isolation, and detachment. The breakaway phenomenon occurs when the pilot, lacking oxygen, wishes to ascend forever.

LOST: Ground,

Guts,

Marbles, Faith, Mind,

Sense and Direction,

Time,

Your Cool, Cool, Heart.

A human loses consciousness at 50,000 ft, bodily fluids boil at 63,000. *The monotone begins with the bird's eye view*, said Malevich. Perspective derives from *perspicere* meaning to see through. Still, we think, to see pain is to have some knowledge of it. To bear witness is to have some effect. The anxiety of a touch under which one fails to rouse. While pilots called this ascent *the breakaway*, deep sea divers called the unending descent through the sea *a rapture of the deep*.

## *Lines that Extend from a Circle and Share a Common End Resemble a Megaphone.*

Polluted air results in clouds with more droplets which increase the ability to reflect light from space. The smaller a drop of water, the more spherical its form in descent. Sudden shifts in scale may signal a nearing. The straight line quickens the pace of the eye while small curves suggest ornamentation. Can the necks of flowers contort in pain? At three thousand feet per second a quarter inch thick plate of steel may be dented by a drop of water. Fragmenting edges and a convex base form dissipating cumulus clouds and *increasingly I miss you*. A raindrop is not tear-shaped. *Horse and cart; fish and water; nothing says I love you like the slope of a warm front gentler than that of the cold.* The vertical divides while the horizontal expands.

# *Houdini!*

Houdini leans to rise from the sofa on which he has been reclining and, in rising, receives a succession of punches to the lower abdomen. Although the magician endured a blow before a small crowd days before, it is here, backstage, in the dressing room at the Princess Theatre that the story of his death is often initiated. Here, backstage, Houdini has been talking with one young man while another uses pen and paper in attempts to capture his likeness. The magician says he can predict the outcome of any detective story given a few excerpts from the book and, to test this claim, the soon-to-be assailant pulls a mystery from his bag. After a few selections are read, Houdini recounts the rest. Then asked by the young man if he might demonstrate the incredible strength of his "iron stomach," the magician, tired and enduring what may be a case of appendicitis, tries to direct Mr. J. Gordon Whitehead's attention to his equally impressive back and forearm muscles against which he invites the twenty-eight-year-old theology student to lay a hand.

Escape relies on a rejection of pain and fear, said Houdini, three days earlier, in a lecture at McGill University. And to demonstrate he stuck a needle through his cheek, which failed to draw blood. Then he added that the imagination inflates suffering. If we really could see, we'd see through these so-called miracles. These were the sorts of claims that had gotten him in trouble with the Spiritualists who believed the living could communicate with the dead through mediums. Houdini considered it a manipulation of those who still mourned the departed. Devoted as he was to exposing fraudulent mediums, he continued to hold out hope that some communication may be made with his dead mother. He created secret code words shared with at least twenty individuals—whoever died first would send the message back to him, thereby bridging the inexplicable terrain between life and death, proof of hereafter.

"Such an agreement I made with both my parents. They died and I have not heard from them. I thought once I saw my mother in a vision, but I now believe it was imagination."

The punches Houdini took to the abdomen backstage on October 22, 1926, would later be considered murder. Or maybe it was the "experimental serum" administered by the doctor in Detroit days later. Houdini didn't know. He knew several Spiritualists wanted him dead, sent him letters to this effect. More often a medium attributed these predictions or threats to a spirit; said spirit guide Pheneas to Sir Arthur Conan Doyle, "Houdini is doomed, doomed!"

. . .

Spiritualism is a movement, a philosophy, a religion, and a science of continuous life that starts in 1848, Hydesville, NY, where sisters Kate and Maggie Fox devised ways to outwit their mother by threading a string through an apple, directing it down the stairs and claiming these thuds were the tracks of a ghost in the dark. They started making sounds by cracking their toes, knees, ankles, and answered these calls from beyond by rapping their knuckles on a table: "Mr. Split-foot, do as I do." Soon their mother was inviting the neighbors over to bear witness to these occurrences. Their older sister Leah then returned from Rochester to form a local "Society of Spiritualists," which she gathered at the house. This is how the Fox sisters came to be called the first modern mediums.

Scientist William Crookes, following an investigation of Kate's abilities, would later say of Ms. Fox:

> . . . it seems only necessary for her to place her hand on any substance for loud thuds to be heard. . . . I have heard them in a living tree — on a sheet of glass — on a stretched iron wire — on a stretched membrane — a tambourine — on the roof of a cab — and on the floor of a theatre. Moreover, actual contact is not always necessary; I have had these sounds proceeding from the floor, walls, etc., when the medium's hands and feet were held — when she was standing on a chair — when she was suspended in a swing from the ceiling — when she was enclosed in a wire cage — and when she had fallen fainting on a sofa. I have heard them on a glass harmonicon — I have felt them on my own shoulder and under my own hands. I have heard them on a sheet of paper, held between the fingers by a piece of thread passed through one corner.

And such was Kate's desire to believe in her own manifestations, that her sister Maggie wrote, in a confession published in the

Sunday edition of the *New York World,* October 21, 1888, "...she told me she received messages from spirits. She knew that we were tricking people but she tried to make us believe. She told us before we were born spirits came into her room..." To leave nothing to the imagination, Maggie took the stage at the New York Academy of Music later that night, slipped out of her right shoe, placed her foot on a wooden stool and began to rap. Of the performance, one woman, now persuaded of their forty year ruse, wrote in from San Francisco: "I know that the pursuit of this shadowy belief has wrought upon my brain and that I am no longer my old self."

Six years following the Fox sisters' first manifestations, the Davenport Brothers began to present evidence of the supernatural in another context—that of their own magic performance. The Brothers were best known for an act in which they both bound their legs and arms and enclosed themselves in a large box on stage. The lights would go down. Then instruments would seem to float through the auditorium. Inspired by the Brothers' ability to slough off their restraints, carry out these sounds, and bind themselves once more in the box on stage, one audience member set about planning his own series of escapes. Some call him the Father of Escapology, some call him the Handcuff King; by simply calling his name one cannot know which is sought: the man himself; or those who followed.

Houdini hangs head first over a crowd in Times Square. With his neck and shoulders curled forward in the straitjacket about his torso, he looks like a hook rising only to be cast. Houdini relaxes. The crane stops. Houdini thrashes about in the air—and after a few seconds, he folds the canvas from his core, dangles it from his right arm. The camera frames only the sky and his form as it follows from crane to straitjacket. Rewind and he has fettered himself again—the restraint an extension, the body a stage. And because the jacket dangles, divested of its power, because the body arches against a cloudless sky, we may assume that those who gaze upon him from beneath the lower frame have sounded their applause and perhaps, we think, they are reaching, though this evidence has not been maintained. Houdini knows the body, knows it's not an instrument for the voice from beyond—could never hold the message for which he waits. Though every voice needs a body that beds a pain, troubles a mind, surely any attempt to structure the ineffable would overwhelm that through which it passes.

Belief must maintain the favor of both one's reason and will. "I am willing to believe," said Houdini when asked about Spiritualism, "but of all I have seen I have never found anything that couldn't be explained by human effort. My mind is open. I am a human being, and I have loved ones on the other side. I would like to get in touch with them if it were possible."

With each shackle he shook from his arms and his ankles, Houdini cast off a name. He escaped from chains, cuffs, cuffs with Bramah locks, Bean Giant cuffs, French Letter cuffs, Rohan's cuffs, Krupp's cuffs of which he said, "I was in that cuff half of an hour and it seemed like an eternity," a Black Maria en route to a prison in Siberia, a galloping horse, a sea monster, a "crazy crib," a giant football, a U.S. mailbag, a fragile paper bag, a wet sheet, a lit cannon, a leather belt, a packing case, a rotating wheel, a rolltop desk, the Water Torture Cell, a hot water boiler, a water mill, a glass box, a "ghost box," the Metamorphosis box, the Milk Can, milk churns, *Mirror* cuffs, an "invincible bracelet," irons, leg irons,

"bridge jumpers," iron boilers, iron-ringed wicker basket, mana-
cles, shackles, straitjackets, sailcloth sacks, safes, cells in Brooklyn,
Buffalo, Cleveland, Detroit, Missouri, and Rochester, cell no. 3 in
D.C., cell no. 2 in D.C. on Murderer's Row, trunks, locked trunks,
roped trunks, snow tires, Boston tombs, diving suits, coffin with
screwed down lid. And Houdini remains in the coffin originally
fashioned for a performance from which, now, forever, he is
expected to emerge.

# *Anechoic*

In this picture my mother wears a strapless black lace ball gown. She is at a round table, looking down at her fingertips playing at the edges of a wine glass. She seems to be in the midst of a story as the men on either side lean toward her like legs of an isosceles triangle. The glass of white wine stands tall before her hands, which linger, dripping their long fingers with large knuckles. These hands angle daintily toward the rim of the glass. I remember how she used to make the glasses whirr. She would pass her index finger quickly along the surface of the wine, then circle the lip of the glass again and again until a magnificent sound came on slowly as if always there, then expanding like a gas, filling every corner of the chandelier-topped banquet hall. She would wink and look the other way once the notes had reached their peak and people at other tables hushed to search the room for an origin.

The voice is intimate: we experience our own voice through a combination of a synthesis of air and tissue conduction; that is, we both hear our voices and feel the vibration of the sound we emit. And this is what I am thinking about as I sit on a red couch in the waiting room at the University of Iowa's Wendell and Johnson Speech Center. In the opposite corner of the room, a mummified child sits in a blue plastic chair. The plaque above the figure indicates that it is the result of a project completed by children with hearing complications. The figure holds a similarly mummified book open in its lap; however its torso and head are extremely reclined, and there is no accounting for a pair of eyes.

Apart from these traces of a world beyond audition, I have come here to explore the second largest anechoic chamber in the United States, built in 1967. A blond-haired woman appears and leads me down two flights of stairs, down to the basement. The stairs end at a thick, heavy door that she pulls open by wrapping her hands around the handle and throwing her body back. Inside, a thre- foot-wide metal catwalk rests on a wire trapeze that bisects the inner structure, which is walled in steel. The ground is the same distance below our feet as the ceiling is above us. The outer structure is made of concrete in order to isolate this room within a room from earth's vibration. The walls, floor, and ceiling are covered in fiberglass wedges designed to absorb sound.

"Hear that?" she asks.

"No, what is it?"

"The whirring of that light above us is so loud. Let me turn it off. Don't worry; I won't shut you in here. It would be too disorienting."

In an anechoic chamber, the only sound that exists is the sound, which derives from a source. In other words, the sound which cannot be accounted for may be an illusion triggered by the brain; this is an environment in which one may find how the body leads itself astray. The first anechoic chamber in the U.S. was built in 1940 at Murray Hill, Bell Labs, and was once cited by the Guinness Book of World Records as the "world's quietest room." I turn away from the door as she goes out to extinguish the light. In the dark, my ears strain to grasp something, but the only thing I hear is a sort of static that could be confused with the mechanism itself. This chamber consists of a steel walled room within a thirty-foot concrete cube. The rooms are separated by a four-inch air space. I pronounce an "h," as if too exhausted to complete the mundane English salutation. It seems to follow as far as my breath endures on exhale.

In 1951, to explore the effect of a lack of external stimuli on the human brain, McGill University psychologist D. O. Hebb conducted experiments on student volunteers. These experiments were devised to limit the subject's ability to perceive his or her own environment. They would lie on a bed in a partially soundproof room within a room. They would lie for hours, days, in the darkness beneath the hum of the air conditioner—their hands and forearms fitted with cotton gloves and cylindrical cardboard cuffs to limit tactile sensation; their eyes covered by translucent goggles to prevent patterned vision, allowing only a hazy light. Each head placed in a U-shaped foam-rubber pillow. If at any point the subject felt he could not go on he could press a panic button.

Although Hebb preferred to use the term "perceptual isolation," many people still attribute "sensory deprivation" to the methods used in his early experiments. Both terms are misleading. While it is possible to deprive the eyes of light, the same cannot be done with hearing. Although a subject may be placed in an entirely soundproof room, there is still the matter of the circulatory system. The subject hears blood coursing through the blood vessels near the ear, listens to the breath rushing through the chest, notices the rumblings of the stomach. There are heart noises, breathing noises, sounds made by the middle-ear muscles. In some cases, they are mistaken for auditory hallucinations, which the subject recognizes as: "dripping water," "typewriter," "howling dog."

Most sensory deprivation subjects in Hebb's experiments indicated that as the test wore on they came to believe that the experimenter had deserted them, but such was never the case. Some subjects reported that they felt as if another body was lying beside them in the cubicle, but such was never the case. One subject drew a picture to show how he felt at one point and said it was as though there were two of me, and was momentarily unable to decide whether he was A or B.

Before leaving the house where my mother died, I went looking for her. There was a sense of stillness in her room that could have been mistaken for order and an order that begged a kind of presence by which absence might be measured. I searched through the hangers around which her blouses and jackets clung tenuously by pale buttons, through the yellow legal pads on which she kept her days' lists. I searched, as if like a paper doll, she was cut from the background of the world and could be found in the space left behind.

.    .    .

After an initial period of sleep in the chamber, Hebb's subject would lapse into daydreaming. Although some had planned to spend the time thinking over some mathematical problem, they quickly found that they could no longer maintain concentration. Their thoughts wandered to the past. They imagined traveling from one land to the next, envisioning each step.

One sensory deprivation subject made up a game of listing, according to the alphabet. For each chemical reaction he would name the discoverer. At the letter *n* he was unable to think of an example. He tried to skip *n* and go on, but *n* kept coming back. *N* demanded an answer. He tried to dismiss the game altogether but he could not. He endured the game for a short time. And finding that he was unable to control it, he pushed the panic button.

Hebb later admitted that his experiments in perceptual isolation were used to explore the effects of brainwashing. His clarification was made ten years later at the 1961 Harvard Symposium on Sensory Deprivation:

> *The work that we have done at McGill University began, actually, with the problem of brainwashing. We were not permitted to say so in the first publishing. What we did say, however, was true ... 'Brainwashing' was a term that came a little later.*

There is a form of soft torture used in the early stages of brainwashing. The effects are seldom discussed. You are the prisoner of war. And the guard hands you a blank sheet of paper. He says; *Write out your autobiography in as much detail as possible.* You write for hours, days. You hand over the record. He thanks you, may commend your attention to detail, the inclusion of a heartfelt affect.

He hands you another sheet of paper. *Write out your autobiography.* There appears to be no end.

*Anechoic* literally means "without echo." The anechoic chamber at Harvard University was the supposed source of inspiration for John Cage's 1952 classic, *4'33"*. In 1951, he entered the room expecting to hear silence. Instead, he claimed to have heard two sounds, one high and one low. The engineer in charge informed Cage that the high sound was his nervous system, the low one was his blood. It was here that Cage realized, "What we require is silence; but what silence requires is that I go on talking."

After inching out onto the wire trapeze, to the middle of the chamber, I ask my guide whether or not the engineer was accurate in his interpretation of the two sounds as the nervous system and circulation system. She looks me squarely in the eyes and replies: "I don't know about silence, I don't work with silence."

In the neurology of the 1930s and 1940s, certain areas of the human cortex were called "silent." In his 1941 book titled *Epilepsy and Cerebral Localization*, neurologist Wilder Penfield writes that these areas of the cortex "are called silent only because it is found that their destruction produces no detectable interference with mental or psychical function. This is due to the replaceability of those areas." In the darkness of the anechoic chamber, I knew it may be wrong to infuse this approximation of silence with meaning or hope, to find comfort in an environment that prided itself on the purity of experience; but here was a place where sound was, at least theoretically, ensured of an origin.

I woke at 4:00 a.m. and tiptoed downstairs to find her bed empty. The covers were thrown back and I noticed the indentation of her body in the mattress had grown smaller. I pushed the swinging door to the small, adjoining kitchen forward until it bumped against something on the other side. I pushed the object forward using the weight of the door and stuck my head through the opening to find her sitting on the floor, surrounded by shards of glass that caught the moonlight from the window and dazzled her sunken outline. She looked up at me then, smiling, and said, "Sorry to wake you, I was just getting a drink of water and the glass slipped." As she spoke, she held her hands up and we watched as they twitched in the air, beholden to no one.

# Acknowledgments

Some of the essays were published in these journals: *Creative Nonfiction, Ninth Letter, Gulf Coast, Bellevue Literary Review, jubilat, Dislocate, 42opus, Squaw Valley Review, Iowa City Arts Council Poetry in Public Project,* and *POOL.* I thank the editors.

Thank you to the following organizations for their support: Ucross, Jentel, Virginia Center for the Creative Arts, Vermont Studio Center, Kimmel Harding Nelson Center for the Arts, and the University of Iowa Museum of Art.

Thanks to my patient readers: John D'Agata, Leslie Sharpe, Wayne Koestenbaum, Sarah Gorham, Thalia Field, Mary Ruefle, Susan Lohafer, Mako Yoshikawa, Caroline Casey, Eula Biss, Robin Hemley, David Hamilton, Bradford Morrow, and April Freely.

# Sources

Rudolf Arnheim, *Art and Visual Perception*

W.H. Bexton, W. Heron, and T.H. Scott. "Effects of Decreased Variation in the Sensory Environment." *Canadian Journal of Psychology* 8, no. 2 (1954), 70–6.

D. Ewen Cameron, "Psychic Driving." *American Journal of Psychiatry* 112 (1956):503. 502–9.

Bernard Comment, *The Panorama*

Jonathan Crary, *Suspensions of Perception: Attention, Spectacle, and Modern Culture*

Jonathan Crary, *Techniques of the Observer: On Vision and Modernity in the Nineteenth Century*

Michel Foucault, *Discipline and Punish*

J. J. Gibson, *Ecological Approach to Visual Perception*

E.H. Gombrich, *Art and Illusion*

E.H. Gombrich, *The Sense of Order: A Study in the Psychology of Decorative Art*

D. O. Hebb, *Essay On Mind*

D. O. Hebb, et al. "Experimental Deafness." *Canadian Journal of Psychology* 8, no. 3 (1954), 152–6.

Woodburn Heron, W.H. Bexton, and D.O. Hebb. "Cognitive Effects of a Decreased Variation in the Sensory Environment." *The American Psychologist* 8, no. 8 (1953).

Sources

Woodburn Heron, "The Pathology of Boredom." *Scientific American* 196 (January 1957), 52–6.

Martin Jay, *Downcast Eyes: The Denigration of Vision in Twentieth Century French Thought*

Rosalind Krauss, *The Optical Unconscious*

Rebecca Lemov, *World As Laboratory*

Robert Jay Lifton, *Thought Reform and the Psychology of Totalism: A Study of Brainwashing in China*

Maurice Merleau-Ponty, *The Visible and the Invisible*

O. Hobart Mowrer, *Leaves from Many Seasons*

Stephan Oetterman, *The Panorama: History of a Mass Medium*

Wilder Penfield, *Epilepsy and Cerebral Localization*

Duane P. Schultz, *Sensory Restriction: Effects on Behavior*

Philip Solomon et al, *Sensory Deprivation: A Symposium Held at Harvard Medical School*

Susan Stewart, *On Longing*

Konstantin Tsiolkovsky, *Collected Works: Vols I–III*

Kirk Varnedoe, *Pictures of Nothing*

# The Author

Ashley Butler was born and raised in Virginia. She has a BA from Columbia University and an MFA from the University of Iowa. Her work has appeared in *Ninth Letter, jubilat, Gulf Coast, Creative Nonfiction,* and *POOL*. She lives in Texas.

*Ji-Soo Park*